The STAR OF DAVID NEEDLEPOINT BOOK

The STAR OF DAVID NEEDLEPOINT BOOK

B. Borssuck

ARCO PUBLISHING, INC.
219 PARK AVENUE SOUTH, NEW YORK, N.Y. 10003

TO
THE MEMORY OF MY DEAR MOTHER,
MY FIRST AND BEST SEWING TEACHER

All designs, needlework, graphs, and line drawings by the author.
Finishing by Frances Bordeleau, Fayetteville, N.Y.
Photography by John E. Unbehend of Photo-Graphic Arts, Syracuse, N.Y.

Published by Arco Publishing, Inc.
219 Park Avenue South, New York, N.Y. 10003

Library of Congress Cataloging in Publication Data

Borssuck, B
  Star of David needlepoint book.

  Bibliography: p. 128
  1. Canvas embroidery—Patterns.   I. Title.
TT778.C3B654   746.4′4   78-32036
ISBN 0-668-04659-7 (Library Edition)

Printed in the United States of America

Contents

SECTION III
—BIBLICAL THEMES

SECTION IV—ANTIQUITY

SECTION V
—CONTEMPORARY

Preface

There is presently a great accent on the subject of ethnic background and it has touched the needle-work field too. The title contains an implied promise to give you tools to design objects, religious and secular, that express a Jewish heritage. It can be a reference book of motifs and alphabets for the professional designer or accomplished needleworker, but most of the examples are projects for the near novice who wants to develop her design abilities.

Subjects related to your own heritage strongly invite you to greater self-expression than you can put into working a predesigned canvas, a sterile occupation compared to defining your own personality and background. Though more hand-painted or printed canvases and kits are now designed for the Jewish-American purchaser, a good selection may not be available to you or appeal to your taste or fill your requirements.

You could—and should—invest more of yourself in your project and thereby reap a greater harvest. The joy and satisfaction of creativity do not come with the kit you buy. Also consider the cost of kits. A package containing canvas, yarn, a graph, and a picture of the finished piece may be as much as three or four times the price of a piece of canvas and yarn to cover it.

You bring an emotional as well as a creative contribution to your needlepoint when you start with a blank piece of canvas, select a subject, dream about it, and visualize it in colors and technique you enjoy using, all before you do a single stitch. Your finished piece will have given you more challenge but will be worth more to you because you have met that challenge. Moreover, it will doubtless be more expressive of your own likes and life style.

Section I is devoted to a formula for executing the Star of David in an endless range of sizes and in a variety of styles and stitches. The pieces shown were done to illustrate the formula, its application, and its versatility. The experienced needleworker will doubtless want to use the *Mogen David* combined with other motifs in more complex designs for home and synagogue, for religious as well as secular objects. The novice can develop designing skills by applying appropriate size stars to small pieces such as pincushions, luggage tags, coasters, headbands, boxes, coin purses, eyeglass cases, cosmetic cases, and picture frames. Make them as gifts for your family and friends or as items to be sold for the benefit of your favorite charitable organization.

In Section II eleven alphabets of different sizes and styles, both traditional and contemporary, will give you great freedom in designing pieces that feature blessings, prayers, or biblical quotations, or commemorate important events in your life.

So with the motifs and alphabets given, you have elements to help you design objects closely related to your religious beliefs and the practice of religious ceremonies in your temple and your home.

The thread of history that runs through the remainder of the book starts with free-form designs that illustrate Genesis in addition to a map of ancient Judea and emblems of the twelve tribes. Simplicity is the keynote of the emblem designs so that they may be within the skills of the near novice, but such simplicity provides those with greater experience and proficiency wide latitude to use them in original ways.

Geometric patterns and borders from the golden age of mosaics in the Holy Land and some patchwork patterns with biblical names that were popular with America's early settlers carry the thread to the final design, modern Israel's official seal, which features the seven-branched menorah (candlestick) described in the Torah.

History is a never ending story and you are part of it as it is part of your heritage. Make it part of your needlework too.

SECTION I

Star of David

INTRODUCTION

Mogen or *Magen David* means Shield or Protector of David. It was not used as a religious symbol in biblical times but has always been closely associated with the Jewish faith. Probably the oldest known representation of the star is in the second-century C.E. synagogue at Capernaum where the decorative motifs also include a *menorah* or seven-branched candlestick, palm branches, and a *shofar* or ram's horn.

In the Middle Ages the Star of David was the emblem of Jewish life in Europe, and in the latter part of the nineteenth century it acquired special political significance as the official emblem of the Zionist movement. It was colored yellow and meant to be a "badge of shame" during the Holocaust, but now the Israeli national flag is a blue, six-pointed star between two blue bands on a white field.

So the Star of David is considered the universal (but not sacred) symbol of Jewish faith and of Jewish people. It is by far the most popular decorative motif used in and on synagogues, on ceremonial objects and furnishings, and on a very large variety of secular objects for the home. You see it in print in organizational literature, in advertisements, on greeting cards, and see it used in an endless variety of other ways.

Geometrically the Star of David is a very simple, very beautiful shape. It is composed of the outlines of two equal triangles superimposed but pointed in opposite directions. It is an easy shape to construct with compass and ruler. When you were a child you probably used your first compass to make six-petal daisies and six-pointed stars.

An equilateral triangle drawn on canvas, however, becomes a series of marks which the needlepointer may find difficult to execute in evenly spaced steps or jogs, for the sixty degree angles of the star do not fall naturally on the square holes of the canvas. By the use of the formula illustrated on the following pages you will ensure a pleasing, symmetrical star of any desired size on any mesh canvas, a star that may be done in a variety of styles and in a wide selection of stitches.

You no longer need to agonize over a hand-drawn outline. Even on canvas, the *Mogen David* should retain an uncompromising directness of line to carry the message of the brotherhood of man expressed by the Shield of David, King of Israel.

STAR OF DAVID BASIC FORMULA

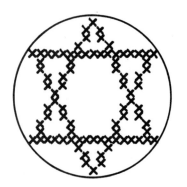

The basic star is done in Cross Stitch.
Each graph square represents one Cross Stitch.
The dark area over two graph squares represents
    two Cross Stitches and indicates the count size.
The crossed circle indicates the center of the star.
There is no limit to the size of the star.
Each point of the star is a single stitch.
Vertical count is always an even number of stitches.
Horizontal count is always an odd number of stitches.

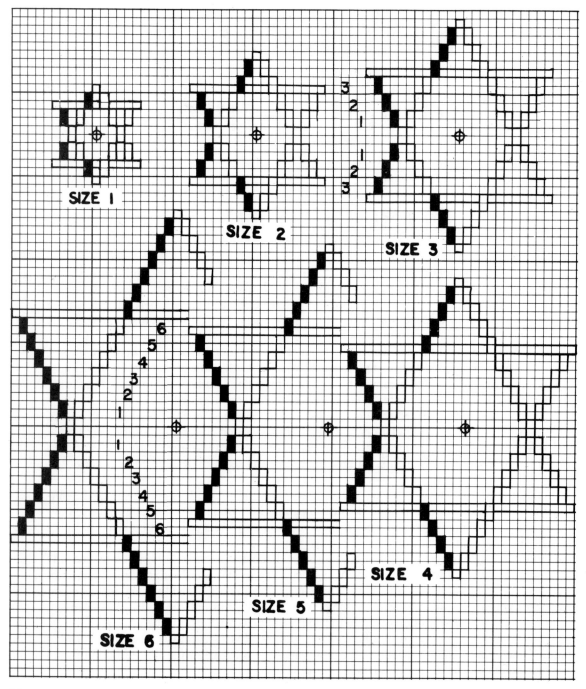

SIZE 1

SIZE 2

SIZE 3

SIZE 4

SIZE 5

SIZE 6

HOW TO ENLARGE BY STITCH

Any design done from a graph may be enlarged by substituting a square pattern of stitches for each square in the graph.

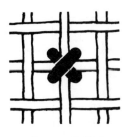

Cross Stitch

Each Cross Stitch in any size star done by the basic formula may be substituted by any of the square patterns shown or by any other square pattern such as a Bargello Stitch unit.

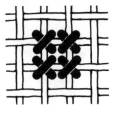 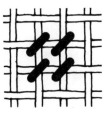 

4 Cross Stitches **4 Tent Stitches** **Mosaic Stitch**

Double Cross or Smyrna Stitch **Rice Stitch** **Upright Cross with Diagonals**

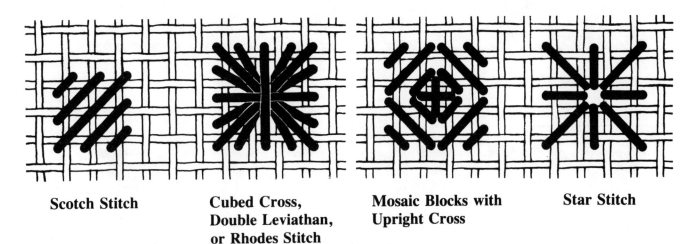

Scotch Stitch **Cubed Cross, Double Leviathan, or Rhodes Stitch** **Mosaic Blocks with Upright Cross** **Star Stitch**

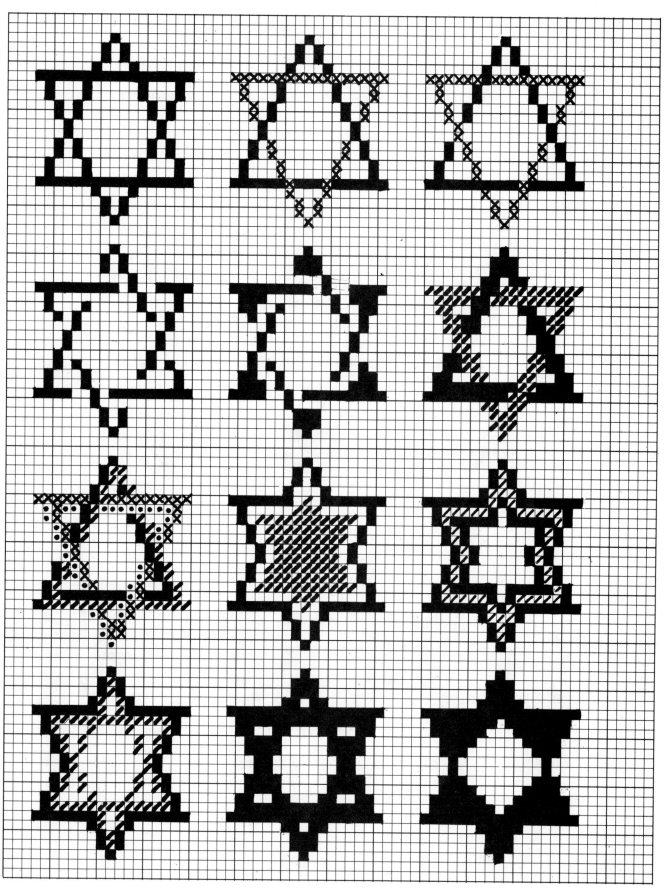

BLUE BOX

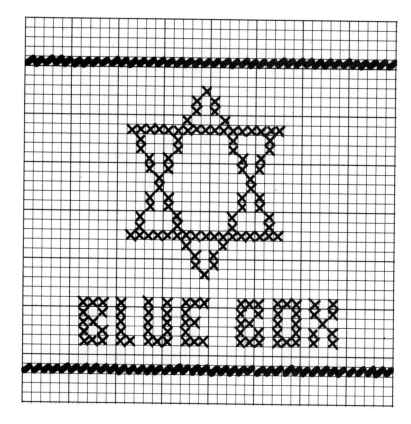

A blue alms box or *pushka* was probably familiar to you in your childhood and still used in your home. This one is a metal band-aid box wrapped in a strip of needlepoint. The bottom of the can was slotted. The hinged end, now the bottom of the bank, facilitates coin removal and renders it reuseable.

DATA

#2 star in Cross Stitch
#12 canvas—3-ply Persian-type Wool
Background—Tent Stitch
Finished size—3¼ x 10

The front and back panel areas may be identical but here the initials RSB are a personal dedication.

WHITE STAR PILLOW

DATA

#2 star on #5 canvas
Yarn—bulky Acrylic
Stitch—Double Cross
Finished size—12 x 12

This piece illustrates enlargement by both stitch and canvas gage. It is white on a bright blue ground but any of the style variations and multicolor effects shown on page 12 could be substituted. Use a larger size star for large latch-needle items such as floor pillows, rugs, or wall hangings.

THREE STAR *TALLIT* BAG

STAR OF DAVID

White Star Pillow—Page 15
Star-in-Square Pillow—Page 18

Three Star *Tallit* Bag—Page 16
Gold Star *Tallit* Bag—Page 20
Blue Box—Page 14

ALPHABETS

Dreidel—Page 43
L'Chaim Pill Box—Page 26
The Ten Commandments—
 Page 27
Chai Sampler—Page 56
Shalom Tray—Page 49

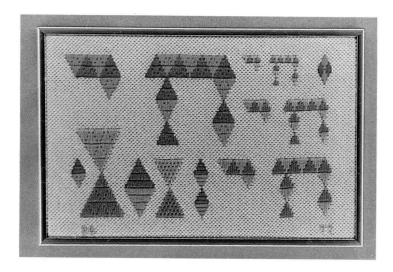

ALPHABETS

Grow-Power *Aleph Bet* Pillow—Page 53
L'Chaim Table Mat—Page 33
Block *Aleph Bet* Pillow—Page 36
Aleph Bet Belt—Page 31

BIBLICAL THEMES

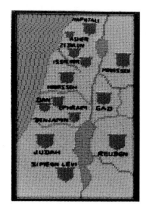

ANTIQUITY

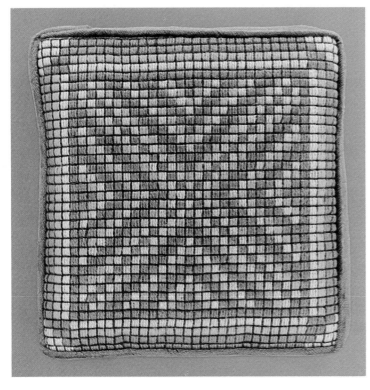

ANTIQUITY

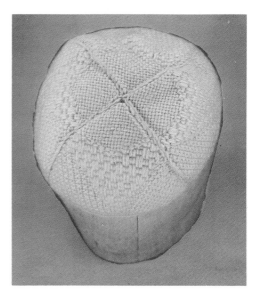

ANTIQUITY AND CONTEMPORARY

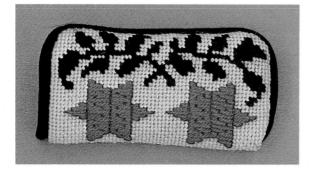

CONTEMPORARY

Knesset Menorah—Page 120
Seal of Israel—Page 122
Hamsa **Pillow—Page 118**
Grape Tray—Page 116

THREE STAR *TALLIT* BAG

DATA

#10 canvas
#1, #4, and #10 star outlines
    Cross Stitch—red Persian-type Wool
Background—Tent Stitch
    Worsted-weight Orlon Acrylic
Finished size—7¼ x 9¼

This piece started out as an exercise in executing the Star of David formula but when the background spaces were filled in with three shades of denim-colored knitting yarns it acquired teenage appeal and became a prayer-shawl bag for a *Bar Mitzvah* gift. Enlarge the background to hand bag, tote bag, or backpack size for a *Bat Mitzvah* gift. Appliqué it on a denim jacket, make it into a pillow or book cover, or add a long fringe to one end for a wall hanging.

STAR-IN-SQUARE PILLOW

DATA

#2 star on #10 canvas
3 strands Persian-type Wool
Background of central area—Tent Stitch
Star and outside border—Scotch Stitch
Narrow diamond frame—vertical and horizontal Bargello Stitch
Finished size—10 x 10
Note: Do the Bargello Stitch diamond before doing the Tent Stitch background.

STAR-IN-SQUARE PILLOW

This is an example of #2 star enlarged by stitch. When bordered by diamond and square it was large enough to make into a box pillow. Though done here in taupe, sand, and white, the design would be equally effective in vibrant, contrasting color combinations.

GOLD STAR *TALLIT* BAG

DATA

#10 canvas

3 strands Persian-type Wool

Letters and center area background—Tent
Stitch

Star—Vertical and Horizontal Gobelin
Stitches, varied lengths

Background—Cross Stitch over two canvas
squares

Finished size—8½ x 8½

This free-form star capturing the richness
of gold bullion embroidery is used on a
prayer-shawl case suitable for the man in
your life. It could also be incorporated into
designs for larger pieces such as Torah man-
tles and ark curtains, either in needlepoint or
embroidered with gold thread on velvet,
linen, or wool fabric.

SECTION II
Alphabets

INTRODUCTION

There are more points of similarity between English and Hebrew letters than appear to the casual reader. The word "alphabet," for example, is from the Greek *alpha* and *beta,* just a step away from the Hebrew *aleph bet* which antedates it. Classic Roman lettering that reads from left to right actually developed from Semitic characters that read from right to left. Mirror-image shapes and heavy vertical strokes instead of heavy horizontal bars account for the greatest differences in appearance between English and Hebrew letters. Scholars can explain and show the changes that come about through centuries, but to a designer or calligrapher the ancient Hebrew *aleph bet* is a source of pure delight.

There are twenty-two letters in the Hebrew alphabet, all consonants. There are additional shapes for each of five letters when they are used at the end of a word. There are no vowels but for children and learners there is a system that uses six combinations of dots and dashes placed over, inside, or below a letter to indicate different vowel sounds.

Written Hebrew words are never divided into syllables and never hyphenated. All lines are of equal length and pages of script have even margins. To make it easier to square off the end of a line, the scribe or calligrapher is given the unique and wonderful ability to s–t–r–e–t–c–h certain letters. The letters that may be expanded are *dalet, hey, het, resh, taf,* final *kaf,* final *peh,* final *mem,* and sometimes *kuf* and *lamed*. Each of these letters "hangs" from a strong horizontal stroke, so horizontal expansion does not affect its basic character or legibility. There are instances in old manuscripts of elongated letters that extend half a page or more, giving unusual style and distinction to the whole.

A selection of sizes of traditional and modern styles were adapted for canvas where possible or given in line drawings for execution in embroidery stitches. Only large sizes of some styles can be graphed. Space is needed to define the lovely curves, but space gives the needleworker areas in which to experiment with color and texture. The small, simple, bold alphabets will be useful for long messages, while the Grow-Power *Aleph Bet* can fill the need for any intermediate size or for very large letters such as are needed in wall hangings or items used to decorate a *bimah* (raised platform in a temple).

The designs in this section are primarily illustrations of the letter styles and shapes as they would look worked on canvas, so most of them are samplers or designs that use short, familiar Hebrew words.

Use the alphabets for biblical quotations and to express your own thoughts and feelings on items that you will want to use in your home; on pillows, wall hangings, rugs, pictures, *tallit* bags, ceremonial pieces or linens for festive occasions, picture frames for *ketubbot* (marriage contracts), *Bar Mitzvah* or *Bat Mitzvah* invitations, wedding and birth announcements, or other memorabilia. Or, working with your friends, design and make a Torah mantle, ark curtain, or wall hanging for your temple or meeting hall.

With the letters of the alphabet at your finger tips, you can say anything.

NAMES OF THE HEBREW LETTERS

Here is the complete Hebrew alphabet. English spellings of the names of the letters vary widely. There is no "correct" way and some alternates are given. Use the most familiar to you in a learning sampler such as shown on page 41.

1. א   aleph (alef)
2. ב   bet (beit)
3. ג   gimmel (gimel)
4. ד   dalet
5. ה   hey (he)
6. ו   vav
7. ז   zayin
8. ח   het (chet)
9. ט   tet
10. י   yud (yod)
11. כ   kaf (khaf)
12. ך   final kaf
13. ל   lamed
14. מ   mem

15. ם   final mem
16. נ   nun
17. ן   final nun
18. ס   samech
19. ע   ayin
20. פ   peh (pe, fe)
21. ף   final peh
22. צ   tzadick (tzadi, zadi)
23. ץ   final tzadick
24. ק   kuf (kof, koof)
25. ר   resh
26. ש   shin (sin)
27. ת   taf (tav)

SIZE 3 *ALEPH BET*

אבגדהוזחט י
כךלמסנןטע
פףצץקרשת

Though too small to be done in needlepoint, this alphabet can be done in embroidery stitches either on fabric or over a needlepoint ground.

SIZE 5 *ALEPH BET*

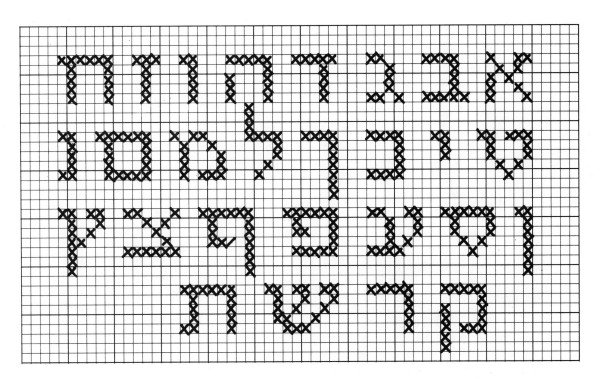

This is the smallest size graphed for canvas. The use of Cross Stitch is recommended so that every letter will retain the sharp angles and clearly defined gaps that characterize modern Hebrew print.

L'CHAIM PILL BOX

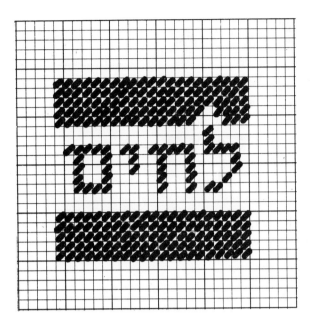

The Hebrew word *L'Chaim* means "to health" and seems appropriate on a pill box.

DATA

Size 5 *Aleph Bet*
#10 Penelope canvas
6-strand embroidery floss
Letters—Cross Stitch
Background—Tent Stitch
Finished size—1 x 1

This little gift item requires very little work. The petit-point piece was trimmed and glued to the top of a plastic pill box of suitable size. Then a picture frame, doll house size, was glued in place to cover the edges of the canvas.

THE TEN COMMANDMENTS

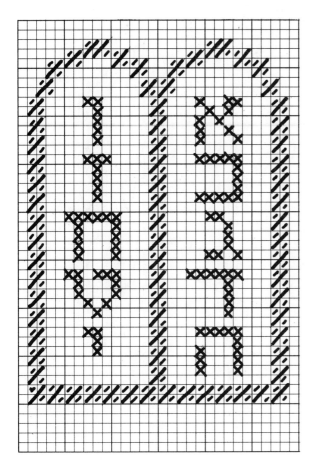

DATA

Size 5 *Aleph Bet*
#14 canvas
Letters—Cross Stitch—#3 Perle cotton
Tablets outline—Mosaic Stitch—#3 Perle cotton
Tablets background—Tent Stitch—#3 Perle cotton
Mat—2 strands Persian-type Wool—Reverse Basket-
     weave Stitch
Frame size—3¼ x 4¼

Either the first ten letters of an *Aleph Bet* or Roman numerals from one to ten are commonly used in small representations of Moses' tablets. Antique gold color and creamy-white Perle cotton contrast with silvery-white wool to simulate the look of parchment and handwoven wool fabric. Frame is gold- and silver-colored. For larger tablets in a design for an ark curtain, for example, use any of the larger size alphabets.

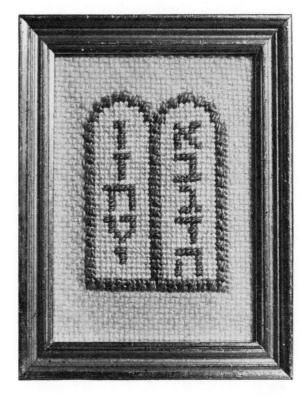

SIZE 7 *ALEPH BET* (OUTLINE)

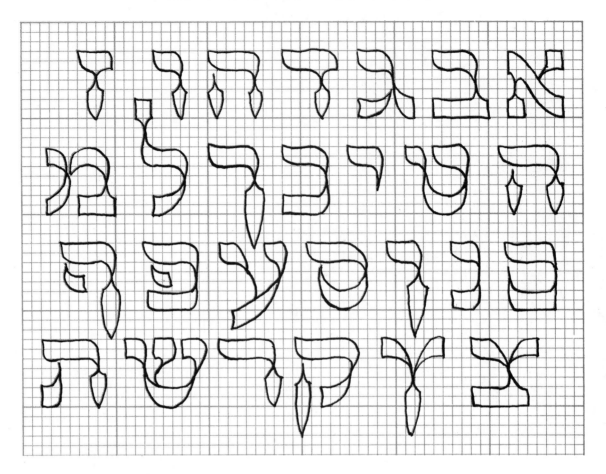

This is a graceful style for embroiderers. Use Outline Stitch only or Satin Stitch only or Outline and Filler Stitches to embellish this "Stam" script, a popular style for religious writings. The graph lines will be helpful for proportional enlargement.

SIZE 7 *ALEPH BET* (GRAPH)

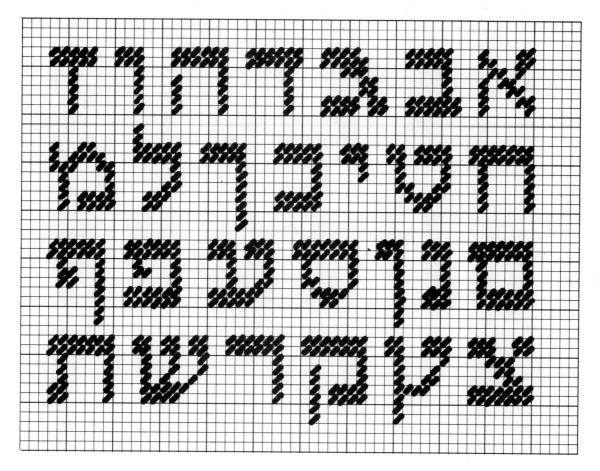

Here is a modern style in a useful size that retains excellent legibility when executed in Tent Stitch.

This design is sharp, bold, and legible when done in Tent Stitch as was used for the belt, but long, slanted stitches over three canvas threads would speed execution without sacrificing legibility or style.

ALEPH BET BELT

The contemporary-style letters of size 10 *Aleph Bet* were used for the red and denim-blue belt, but sizes 5 or 7 could be substituted if a narrower belt is desired. The five final letters (*kaf, mem, nun, peh,* and *tzadick*) were eliminated, leaving one ascender (*lamed*) and one descender (*kuf*) to break into the borders of the belt. Only one stitch separates each of the twenty-two consonants with but one exception. There are two stitches between *vav* and *zayin*, the sixth and seventh letters counting from the right hand end of the belt.

DATA

#10 canvas
Worsted-weight Acrylic
Stitch—Tent
Lettered portion—22½ long
Finished Belt—1½ x 28

31

L'CHAIM TABLE MAT

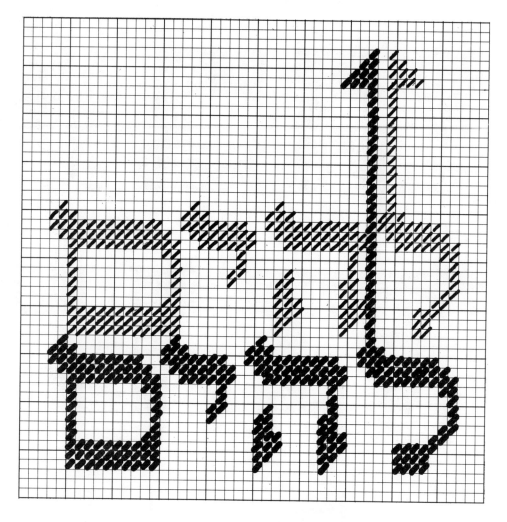

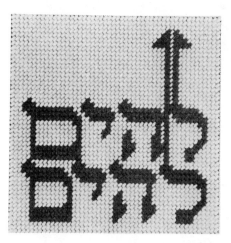

Using a style inspired by old manuscript calligraphy, this design illustrates horizontal and vertical expansion of certain letters to maintain equal borders. The letter *lamed* will stretch both vertically and horizontally, the letter *mem* horizontally only. See the introduction to Section II for the complete list of letters that may be treated in this manner.

A mat for use under your wine decanter says "To your health." The simplicity of the design makes it adaptable to many other items. Use any size or style *aleph bet* and rescale for large, square pieces such as pillows. Extend the ascender of the *lamed* for rectangular wall hangings or rugs.

DATA

#7-mesh plastic canvas
4-ply Acrylic knitting yarn
Stitch—Tent
Finished size—8 x 8

SIZE 15 *ALEPH BET*

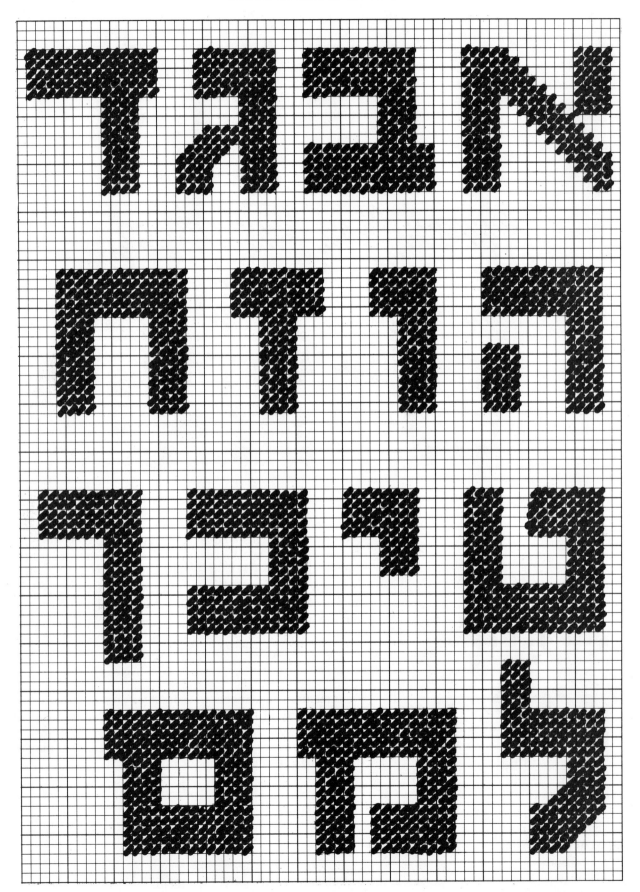

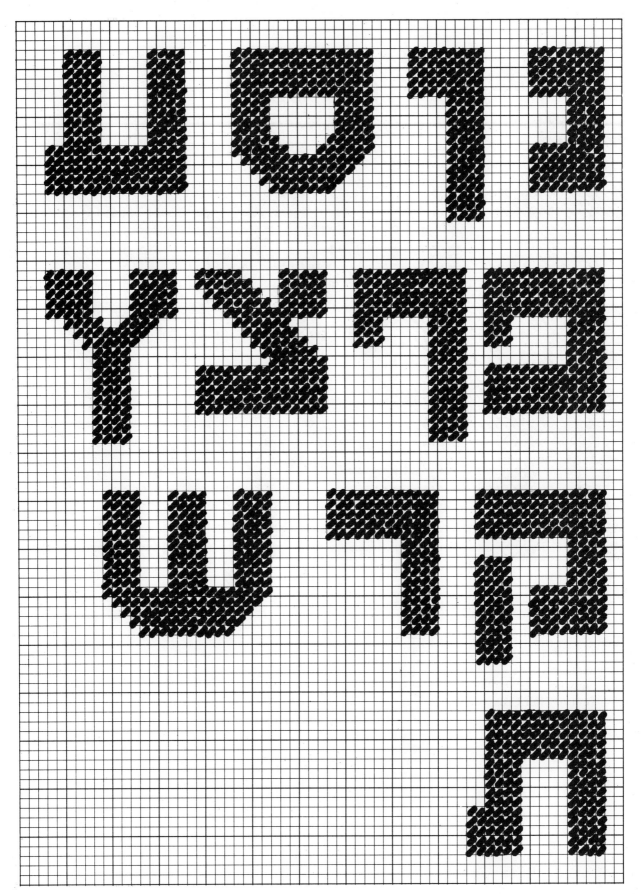

BLOCK *ALEPH BET* PILLOW

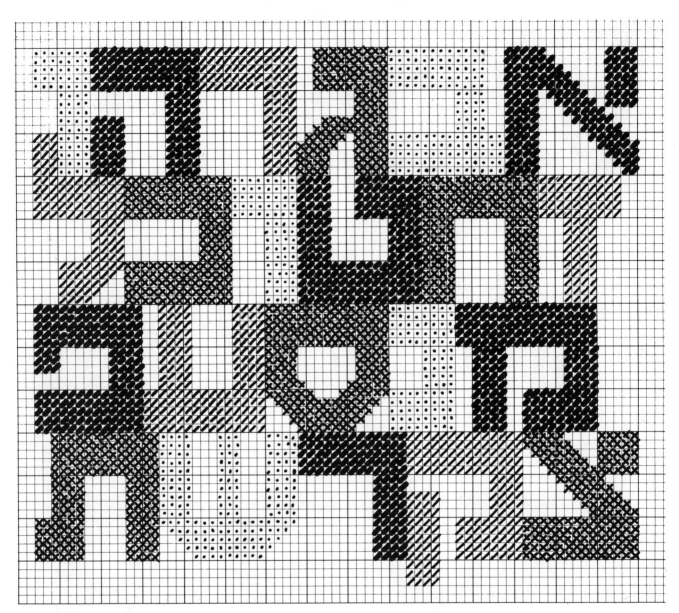

DATA

#5 canvas
Acrylic rug yarn
Stitch—Tent or Half Cross
Finished size—13 x 16

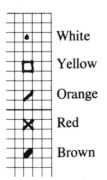

•	White
▢	Yellow
╱	Orange
✕	Red
◖	Brown

BLOCK *ALEPH BET* PILLOW

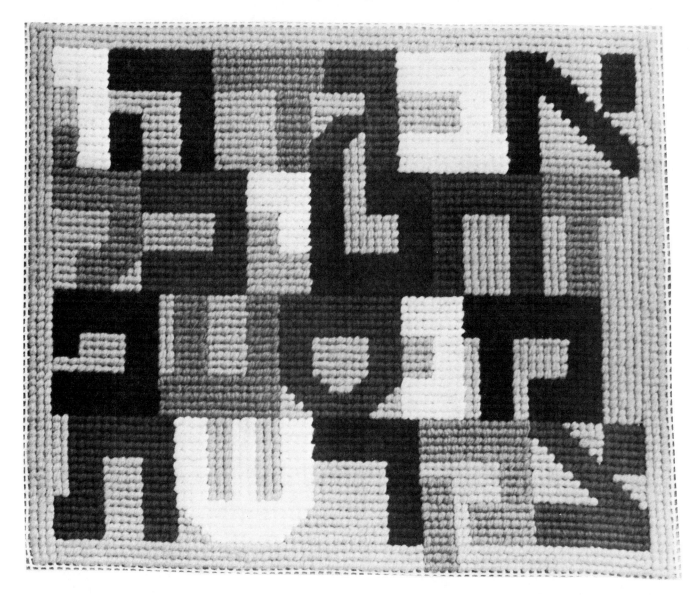

Block letters touch each other to keep background to the minimum in this bold design for contemporary interiors or a boy's bunkroom. Photographic limitations dictated the choice of colors for the illustration but you could use bright, contrasting colors or very subtle shadings with equally effective results.

On #10 canvas, four stitches for every square of the graph for the pillow will result in the same size piece with finer texture, but on #4 canvas four stitches for every square of the same graph will make a rug approximately 23 x 40.

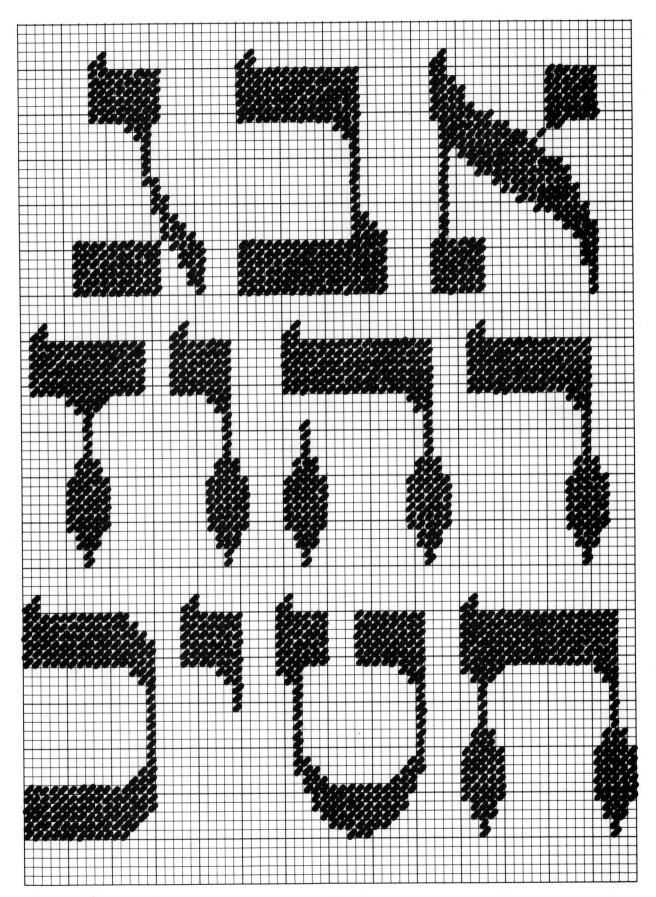

SIZE 25 *ALEPH BET* (CONTINUED)

Here is a style that captures the graceful lines of a quill's thick and thin strokes, especially when done in petit point.

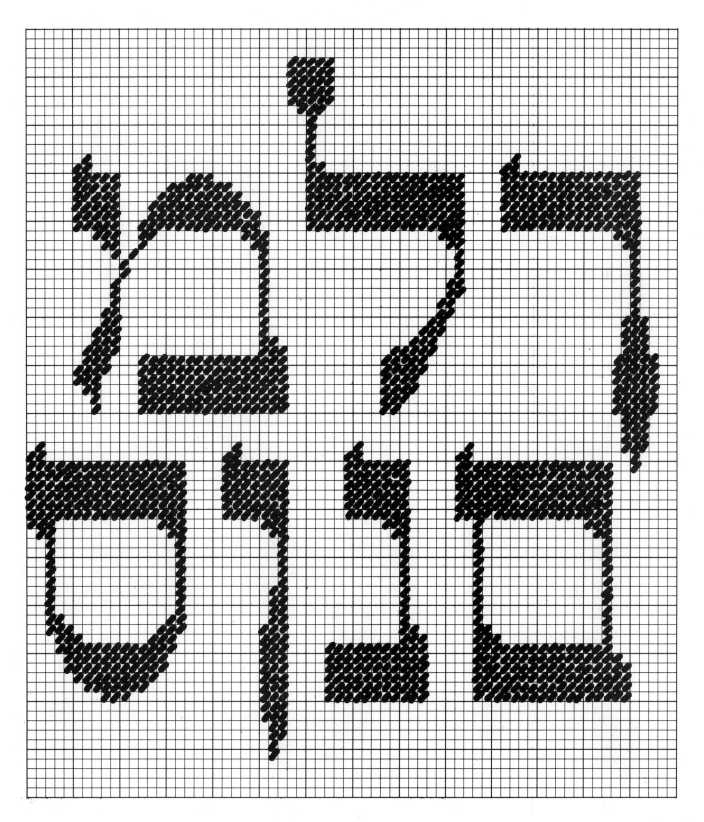

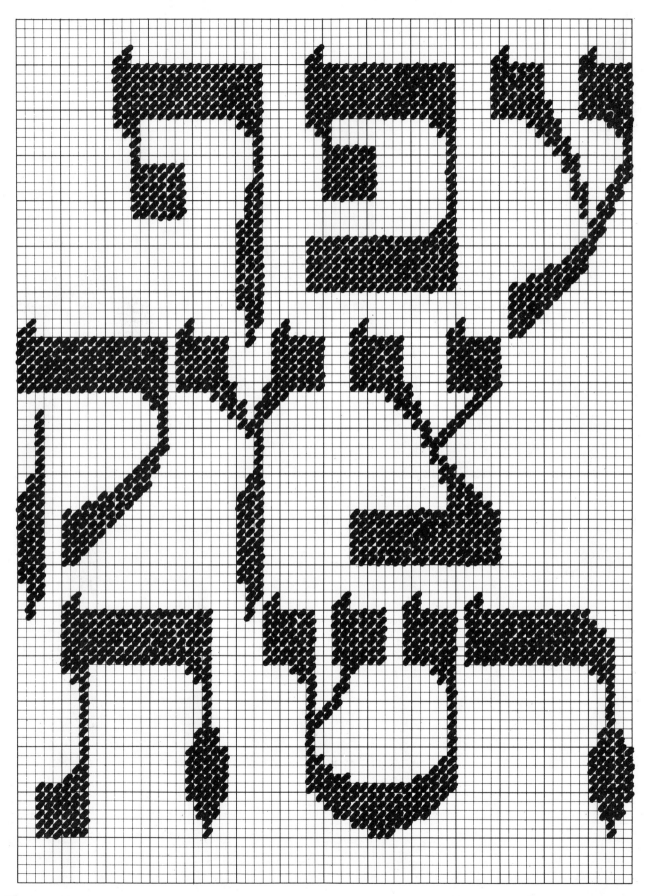

SAMPLER DESIGN

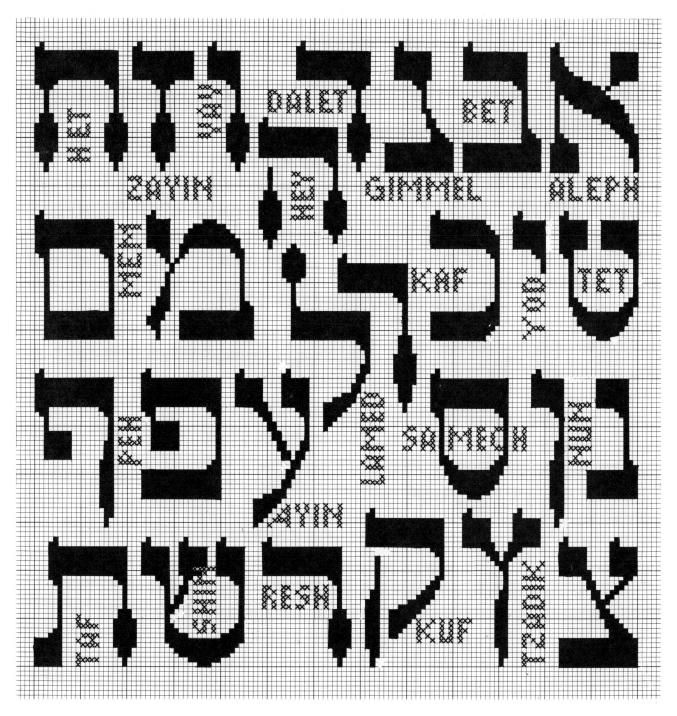

We have here an *aleph bet* sampler with the names of the letters in English to give it additional educational value while creating background interest in the design. Use the larger scale graphs of the individual letters of the size 25 alphabet and the names of the Hebrew letters.

NAMES OF THE HEBREW LETTERS (GRAPH)

Some alternate spellings are included so that you may use those more familiar to you. Cross Stitch is recommended for this size to maintain good legibility.

ALEPH
ALEF
BET BEIT
GIMMEL
GIMEL
DALET
HEY HAY
VOV
ZAYIN
HET CHET
TET
YOD YUD
KAF

LAMED
LAMMED
MEM
NUN
SAMECH
AYIN
PEH PEY
TSADIK
TSADI
KUF KOF
RESH
SHIN
TAF TAV

DREIDEL (SPINNING TOP)

Hanukkah or *Chanukah* (Festival of Lights) celebrates the victory of Judah the Maccabee. It is a joyous holiday and in the old days the children, after a satisfying meal, would gamble with each other for sweets, nuts, raisins, and dates. A spinning top was used. By the rules, each player would spin the *dreidel* and when it came to rest the letter on the top face determined the player's gain or loss.

Nun—player does nothing.
Gimmel—player takes the pot.
Hey—player wins half the pot.
Shin—player contributes to the pot.

To make a large, soft toy shaped like a *dreidel,* use #5 canvas and execute in gros point or with latch needle for a shag texture.

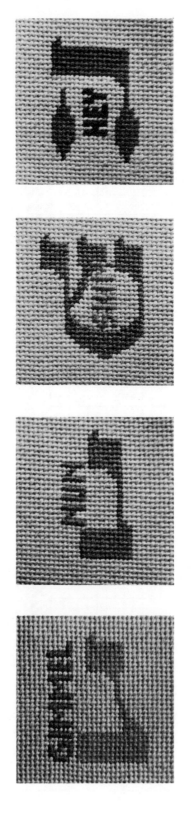

DATA

Size 25 letters on #10 canvas
3 strands Persian-type Wool
Letters and background—Tent Stitch
Names of letters—Cross Stitch—2 strands
    Persian-type Wool
Each panel—3½ x 3½

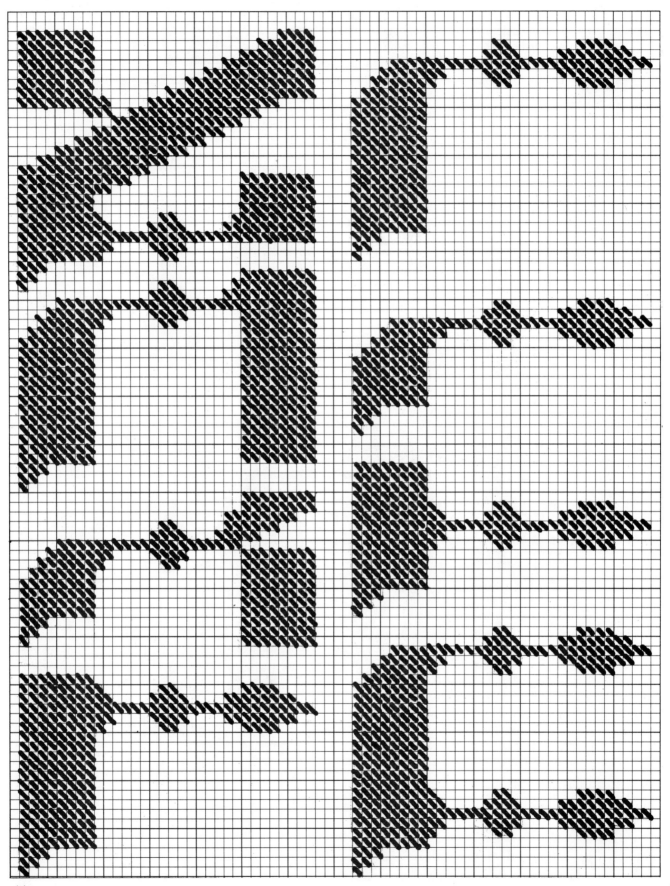

SIZE 32 *ALEPH BET* (CONTINUED)

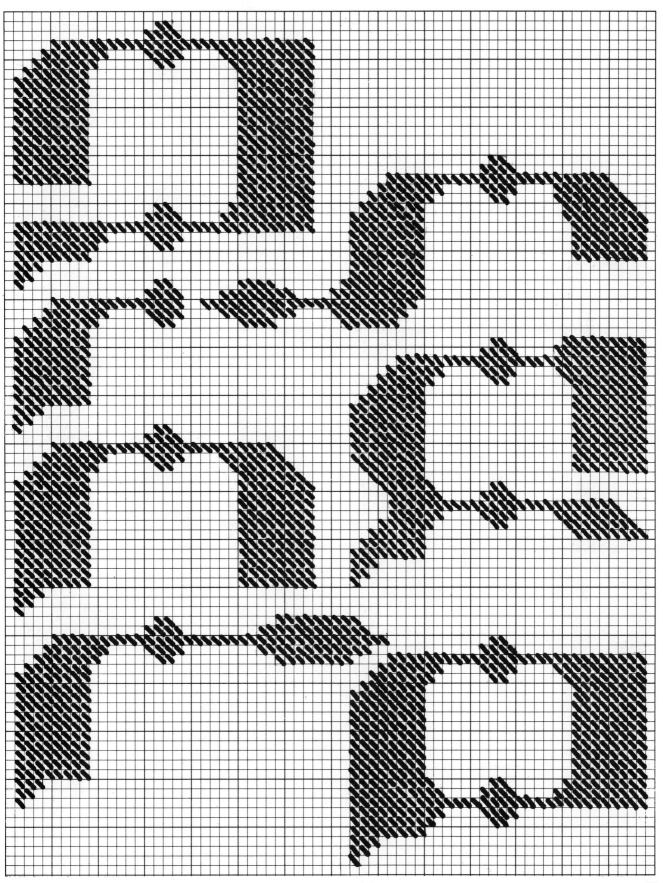

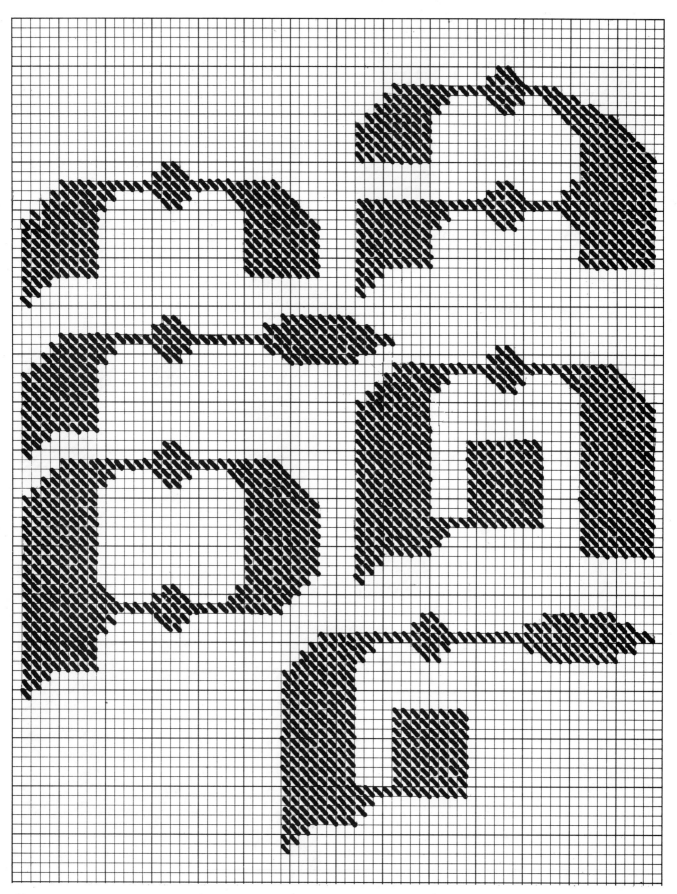

SIZE 32 *ALEPH BET* (CONCLUDED)

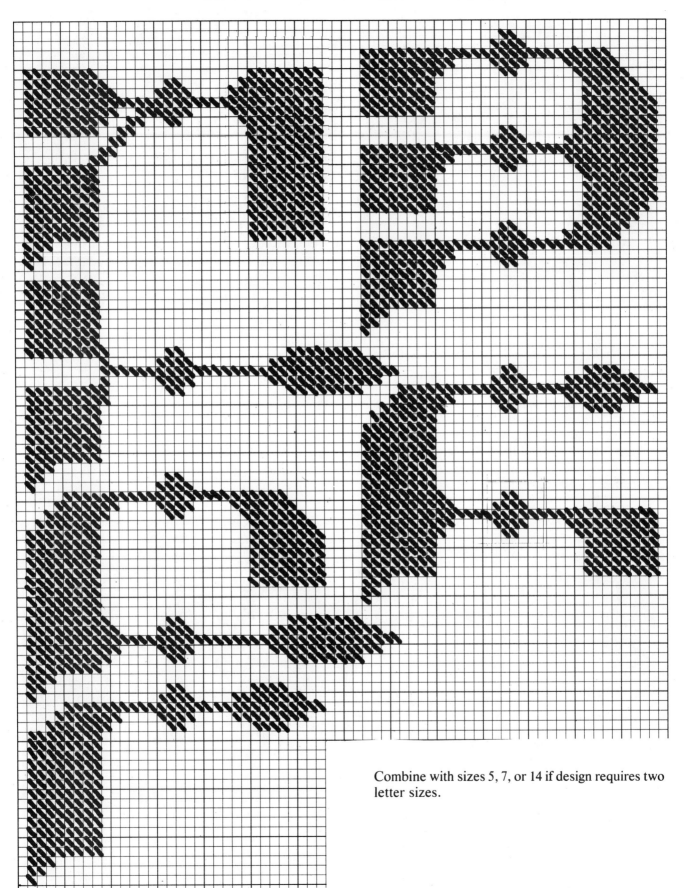

Combine with sizes 5, 7, or 14 if design requires two letter sizes.

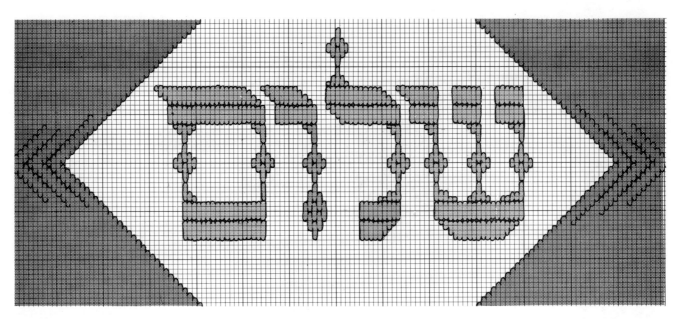

DATA

#12 canvas
Letters—Vertical Gobelin Stitch
        3 strands Persian-type Wool
Corners—Vertical Bargello Stitch
        3 strands Persian-type Wool
Background—Horizontal Brick Stitch
        2 strands Persian-type Wool
Finished size—5 x 12

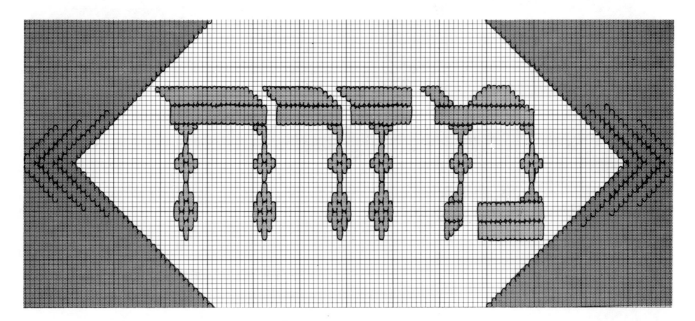

Substitute the word *mizrah* (east) to make a wall placque.

SHALOM TRAY

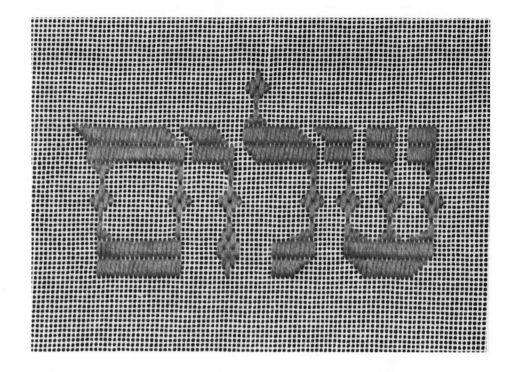

Inspired by letter styles popular in illuminated manuscripts of the thirteenth century, size 32 *aleph bet* gives the adventuresome needleworker space in which to experiment with stitch, color, and texture.

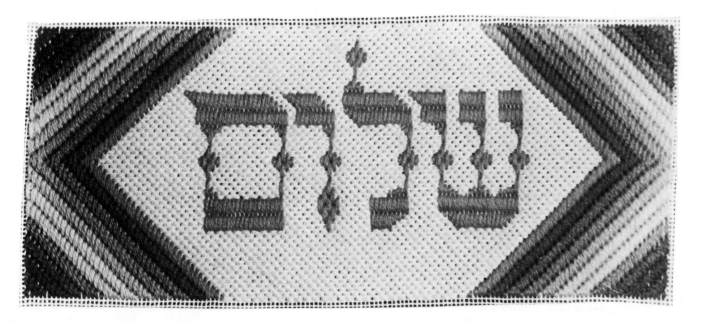

Use *Shalom* (peace or welcome) for placque, tray, or door stop, or make a 12-inch-square pillow by extending right and left corners until they meet and lengthening the ascender of the letter *lamed* up into the triangular space that results.

GROW-POWER *ALEPH BET*

This unique alphabet can fill all your requirements for letters sixteen canvas threads high or higher, even to the banner sizes that would be legible to an entire congregation from the *bimah* (raised platform in a temple). Since letters can be done in any size between these two extremes, this alphabet is particularly suited to a project that requires varied sizes of the same letter style.

Think of these letters as being composed of units or modules rather than single stitches, units that you may enlarge at will in a variety of ways.

The smallest possible unit is made up of three parallel stitches. The middle stitch covers four canvas threads, and the stitch on either side of the middle stitch covers two canvas threads to form a diamond. In a graph the basic unit encloses eight squares (see A and B).

The apex of the diamond may be at the top or at the bottom (see C).

In a graph the basic unit is shown solid black when the apex is at the top, in outline when the apex is at the bottom (see D).

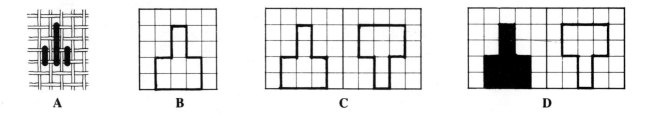

A   B   C   D

The alternating black and white shapes make the graph much easier to read and **do not** indicate different-colored yarns.

Units may touch at any point or any side of the diamond (see E).

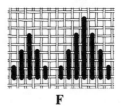

E

Enlarge the basic unit to enlarge the letter size. This may be accomplished by increasing the number and length of the stitches within a unit; always an odd number of stitches over an even number of canvas threads in steps of two threads (see F).

F

The length of the longest stitch in a unit should be determined by the project, the use to which it will be put, the canvas gage, and the type of yarn used. Your own good sense will help you make this decision, for obviously very long stitches that would catch and snag if used on a pillow could be used on a wall hanging that will not be subjected to the same kind of wear.

The *Chai* Sampler illustrates how you may keep the longest stitch within the limits you set, while limitless enlargement of the whole letter is accomplished by using units that are themselves made up of units, either basic size or larger.

The Grow-Power *Aleph Bet* Pillow shows all twenty-seven letters done in the basic three-stitch unit while the *Chai* Sampler shows examples of the grow-power principle.

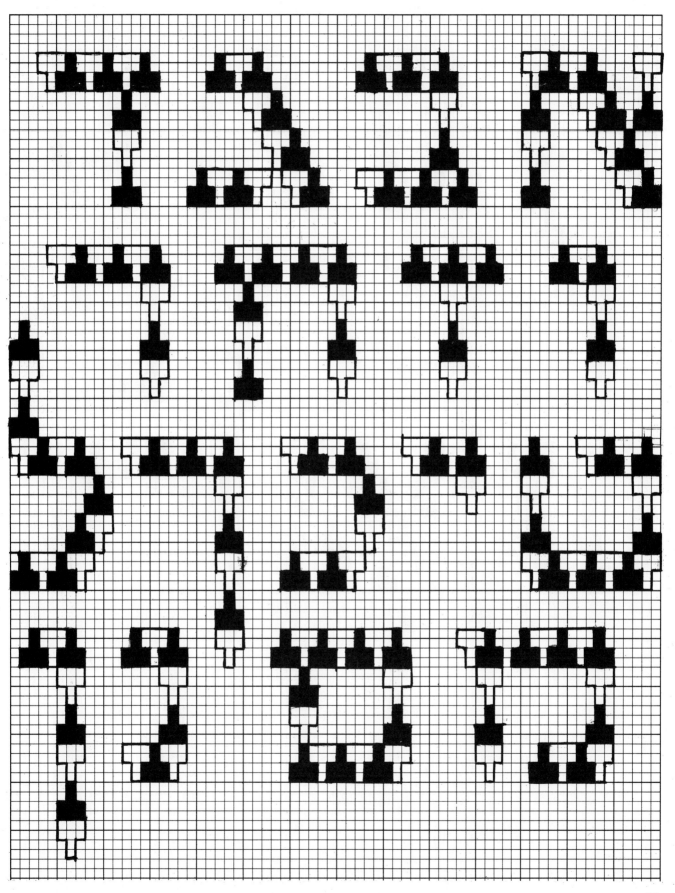

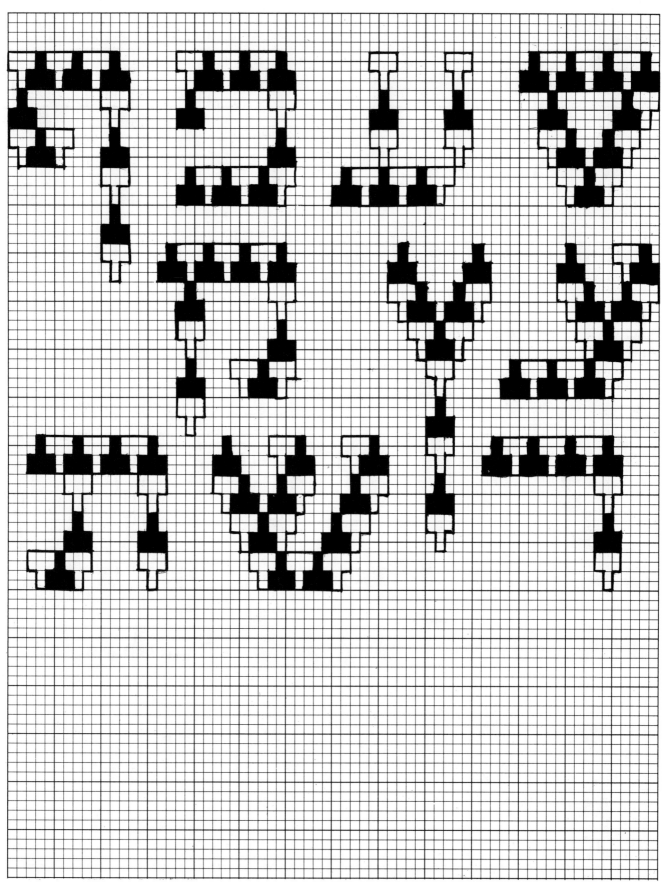

DATA

#12 canvas
3 strands Persian-type Wool
Letters—3–stitch basic unit
Background—Vertical Brick Stitch
    over 4 threads
Finished size—11¾ x 12

This pillow design uses letters done in the Grow-Power basic unit as shown in the alphabet graph but the stitchery shows the true shape and proportions of each letter.

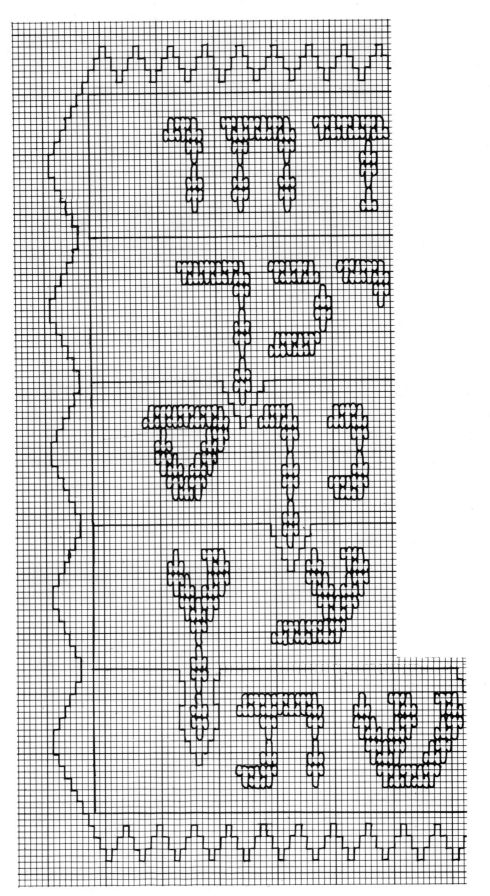

GROW-POWER *ALEPH BET* PILLOW (CONCLUDED)

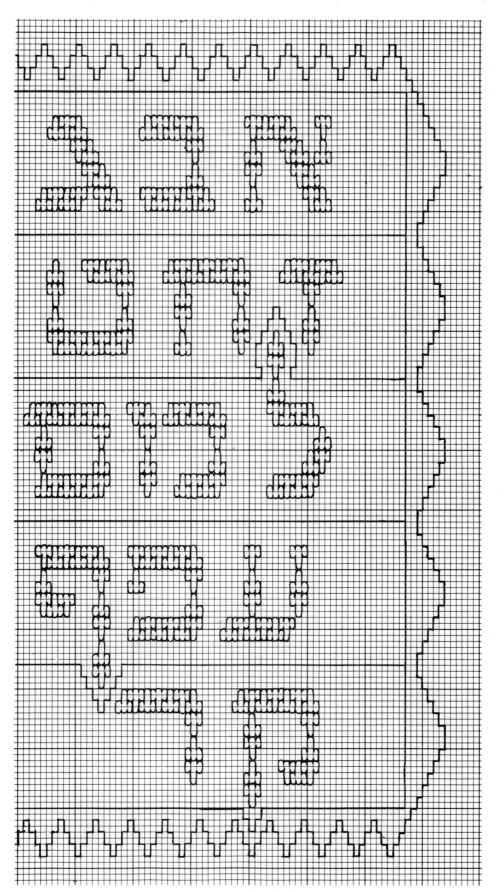

CHAI SAMPLER

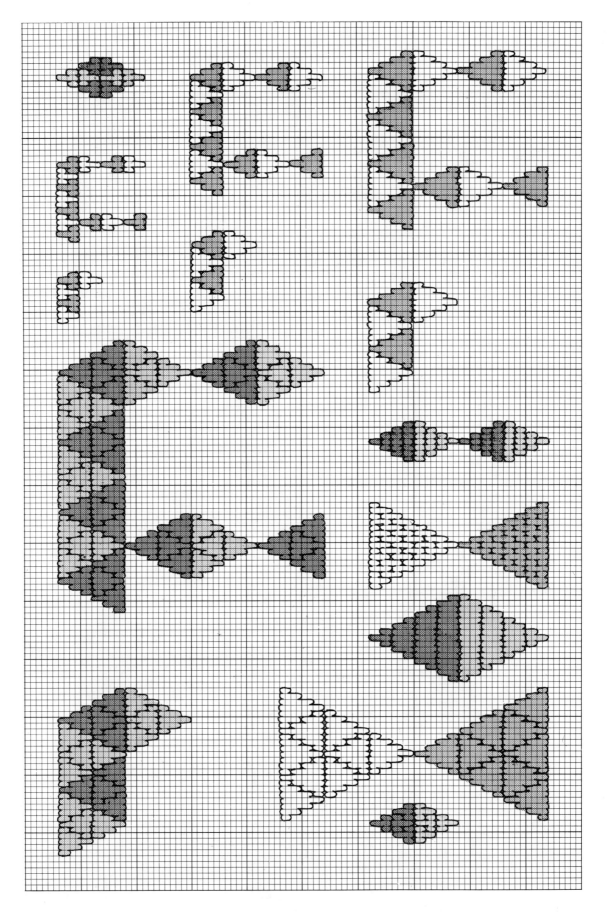

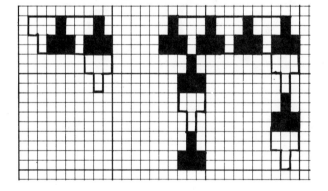

DATA

#12 canvas
3 strands Persian-type Wool
Letters—various Bargello Stitches
Frame size—9 x 14

The word *Chai* (life) is shown graphed in the basic black and white units of the Grow-Power *Aleph Bet*. In the sampler all units with the apex at top are darker in color than units with the apex at bottom for easier identification of individual units. Four sizes of the word for life plus pairs of enlarged units illustrate the growth potential of a single unit and some of the ways in which to execute it.

The smallest possible size using the 3-stitch basic unit is shown in the upper right-hand corner of the sampler. The next two sizes use 5-stitch and 7-stitch units. These are shown along the right hand margin. The large *Chai* in the top left-hand corner is composed of units made up of four 5-stitch diamonds nested together. To make it twice as large again, use the units in the hour glass shape directly below it, units made up of nine 7-stitch diamonds. The other motifs will result in intermediate sizes.

The size to which a unit may be built up is limitless. Yet, as the sampler proves, the letters always retain the shape and proportions of the smallest size.

CROWNED *ALEPH BET*

This alphabet for embroiderers was inspired by the Ashkenazic style of script. The three crown-like strokes are called *tagin*. They are used only on the letters *gimmel, zayin, tet, nun*, final *nun, ayin, tzadick*, final *tzadick,* and *shin*. The center stroke of a *tag* (singular of *tagin*) is usually slightly higher than the other two. On secular objects the designer may rearrange the heights of these decorative flourishes to suit the composition.

Do these letters in gold and silver, royal purple, ruby, and emerald for the rich, jeweled look the crowns demand.

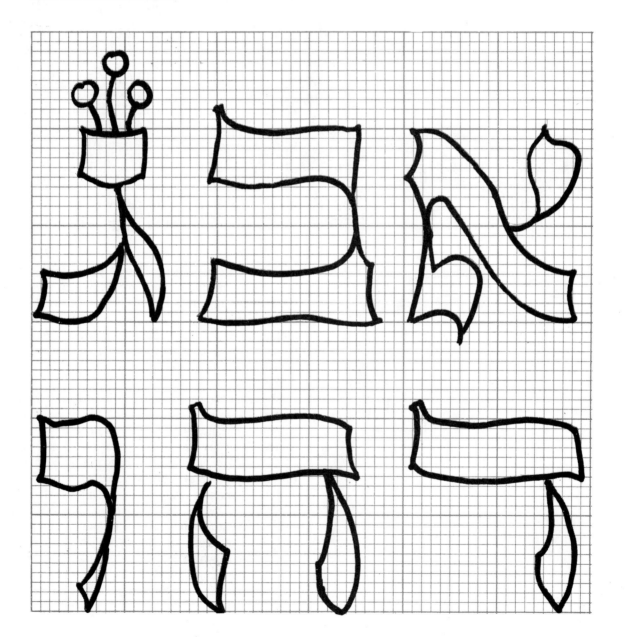

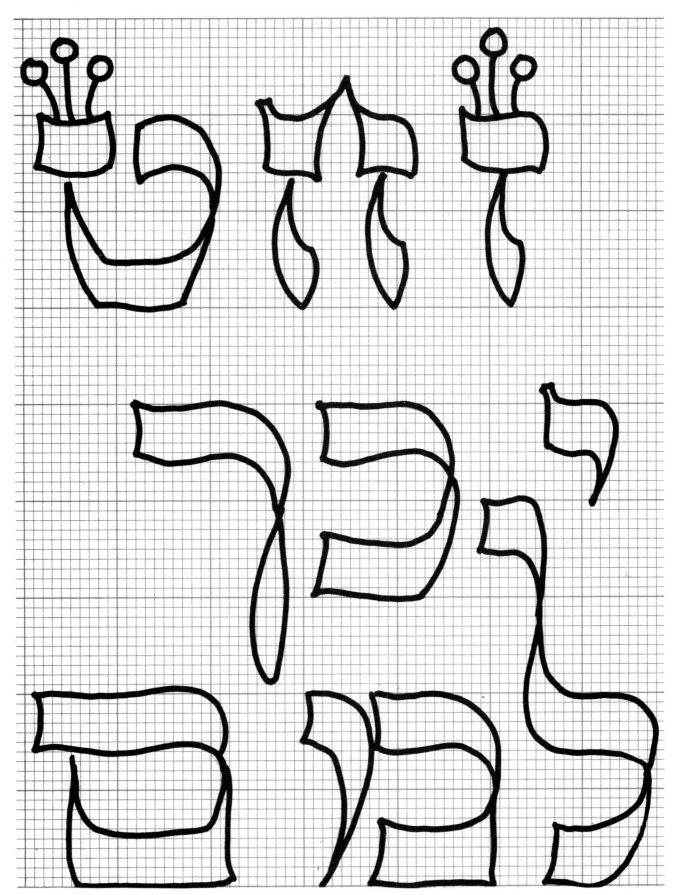

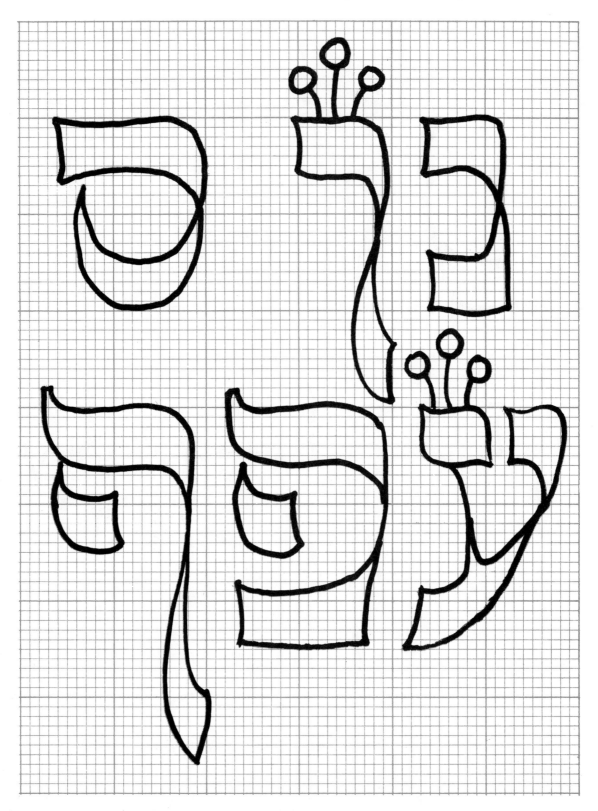

In this style the base line of the letters *tzadick* and *peh* is usually below that of the other letters in the alphabet.

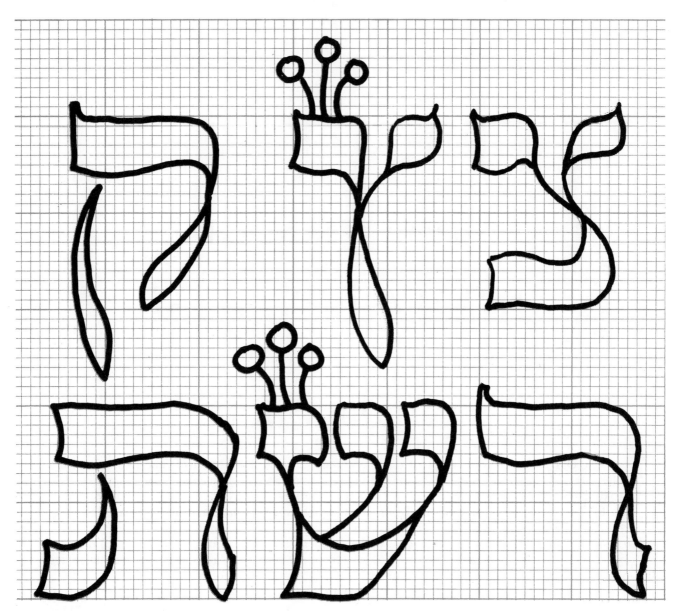

SECTION III
Biblical Themes

INTRODUCTION

The Old Testament is living proof that literary art survives all other artistic endeavors. Scholars believe that it was started before the tenth century B.C.E. and was declared complete and canonized approximately one hundred and fifty B.C.E. It is in three distinct sections, the first of which is the Pentateuch—the five books of Moses—the Torah. This section concerns the commandments and laws that still guide those seeking justice, truth, and peace.

The second section contains the Books of the Prophets and the third contains the Psalms, Proverbs, and five *megillot* (stories), a treasure trove of tales that have echoed and re-echoed in the masterpieces of poets, dramatists, painters, and sculptors throughout the golden ages of each of these arts.

The stories of Adam and Eve, David and Goliath, Noah's Ark, Jonah and the Whale, the Walls of Jericho, the Tower of Babel, and Samson and Delilah have delighted children of many faiths, in many lands, through many centuries. But the recent findings of archaeologists studying the stories in their research indicate some truthfulness in chronicles that seemingly had no foundation in fact.

This is a secular book, a book of ideas and reference material of designs for needleworkers with a Jewish heritage. It is not the time or place for a dissertation about the Holy Scriptures, but a few words about the historic background of each of the designs in this section might bring more interest, emotional gratification, and spiritual investment to the process of pulling your threaded needle through the holes in your canvas.

The Book of Genesis describes the process of creation. Your "In the Beginning" design can be your own first step toward reaping the dividends of creativity.

The Book of Exodus tells the story of "The Passover" from Egypt which is retold every year to the four sons. The fourth book, the Book of Numbers, relates that on the first day of the second month in the second year after the Children of Israel came out of the land of Egypt, Moses was told to take a census of the congregation with the help of twelve princes, one from each tribe.

An emblem for each of the twelve tribes is included here. All are the same size so that a wall hanging of all twelve could be a group project for your sisterhood; or a threesome combining a tribal emblem, the map of Ancient Judea which shows the area in which each tribe settled, and the Seal of Israel would make an attractive grouping for your wall.

IN THE BEGINNING PILLOW

In the beginning God created the heaven and the earth (Genesis 1:1).

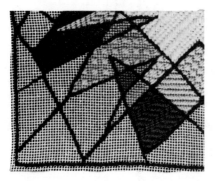

It seems appropriate to start this section with a piece that invites you to step into a new world of self-expression. Express your mood of the moment by fragmenting any given space because any arrangement of colors in odd shapes will be a successful "In the Beginning." Draw the outlines on your canvas and cover them with a dark yarn, using any stitch you desire. Fill in the spaces with colors. Here is an opportunity to use up leftover yarns and to learn new stitches. Your own "In the Beginning" can be a stitch sampler as well as your design first.

DATA

#10 canvas
Stitch sampler
3 strands Persian-type Wool
Finished size—12 x 15

EVENING AND MORNING PILLOW

And God called the light Day and the darkness He called Night.
And there was evening and there was morning, one day (Genesis 1:5).

DATA

#15 canvas
Florentine pattern over 4 threads
2 strands Persian-type Wool
Finished size—13 x 14

The warm colors of a sunlit world and the blue-greens of a cool evening follow gentle curves that suggest water waves, and the beginning of order in the newly created world. If your "In the Beginning" piece introduces you to self-expression in design, consider this piece an exercise in the use of color. The open spaces may be used for any personal message or sentiment.

MAP OF ANCIENT JUDEA

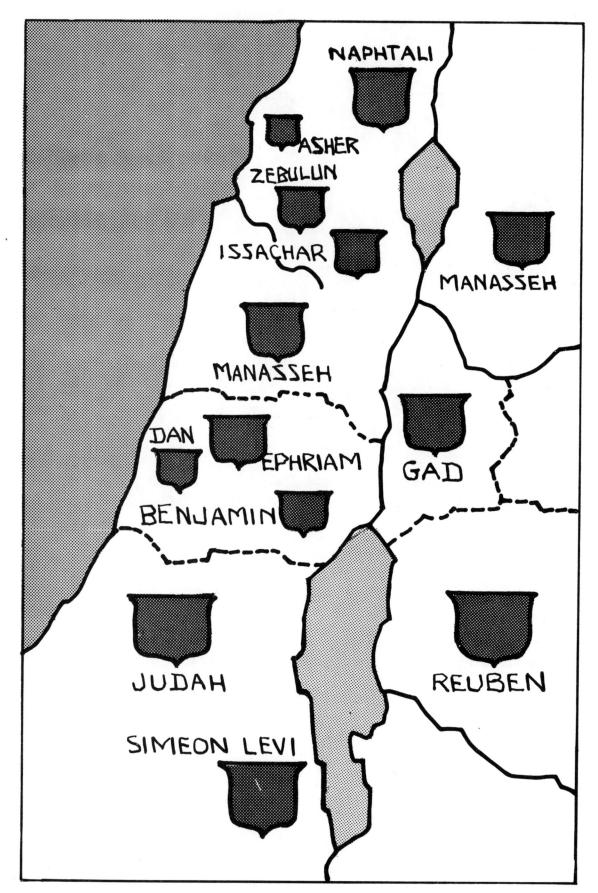

MAP OF ANCIENT JUDEA

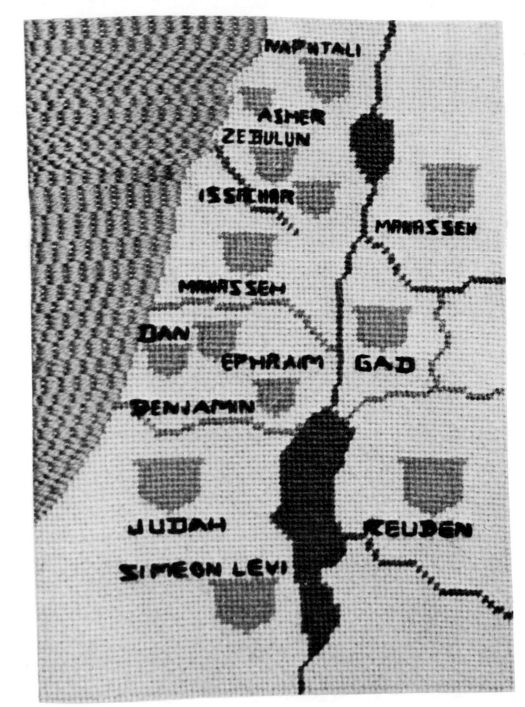

Naphtali
Asher
Zebulun
Issachar
Manasseh
Dan
Ephraim
Gad
Benjamin
Judah
Reuben
Simeon Levi

DATA

#14 canvas
Tent Stitch—2 strands Persian-type Wool
Horizontal Bargello Stitch—3 strands
    Persian-type Wool
Letters—1 strand Persian-type Wool
Frame size—6 x 9

Here is a map of ancient Judea and a corner of the blue Mediterranean. The broken lines in the drawing denote boundary lines and were executed in a darker shade of the ground color, while the unbroken lines denote rivers and lakeshore-lines and were done in green. The names of the tribes were embroidered over the finished needlepoint background.

TRIBAL EMBLEMS

DATA

#14 canvas
2 strands Persian-type Wool
Emblem—Tent Stitch
Names—Cross Stitch
Mat—Diagonal Scotch Stitch
Frame size—8 x 10

Though only one of the twelve emblem designs is shown in needlepoint, all may be done in the same manner, stitch, and colors, or in colors of your own choice.

TRIBAL EMBLEMS

Judah, meaning ''Praise to the Lord,'' was the fourth son of Jacob and was the founder of the tribe which took the leading role in the life of the Israelites.

The tribe of Asher, Hebrew for ''happy'' or ''blessed,'' settled in the Plain of Jezreel. ''More than all the children be Asher blessed.''

TRIBAL EMBLEMS

Benjamin, which means "son of the right hand," was Jacob's twelfth and youngest son. He was founder of the war-like tribe from which Saul, first king of Israel, was a descendent.

Dan was the founder of the tribe known for its fighting men.

Gad means "fortune." The tribe of Gad settled east of the Jordan and later supplied David with some of his best warriors.

TRIBAL EMBLEMS

Issachar means "reward bringer" and was the founder of the tribe that settled west of the Jordan near the Sea of Galilee.

TRIBAL EMBLEMS

Joseph, meaning "God will add," was the favorite son of Jacob and was given a coat of many colors. Sold into slavery by his jealous brothers, he later gained the office of governor of Egypt.

The tribe of Levi received no allotment of land but was set apart to become the teachers of the ordinances of the Lord.

TRIBAL EMBLEMS

The tribe of Naphtali, the tenth son of Jacob, was alloted territory north and west of the Sea of Galilee. He was "like a fleet hind" and the name means "my struggle."

TRIBAL EMBLEMS

Reuben was the first born of Jacob and Leah, ''unstable as water.'' His name means ''behold, a son.'' The tribe of Reuben raised cattle and sheep.

The tribe of Simeon, second son of Jacob and Leah, eventually merged with the dominant tribe of Judah.

TRIBAL EMBLEMS

The tribe of Zebulun ''shall dwell at the haven of the sea.'' The name means ''habitation.''

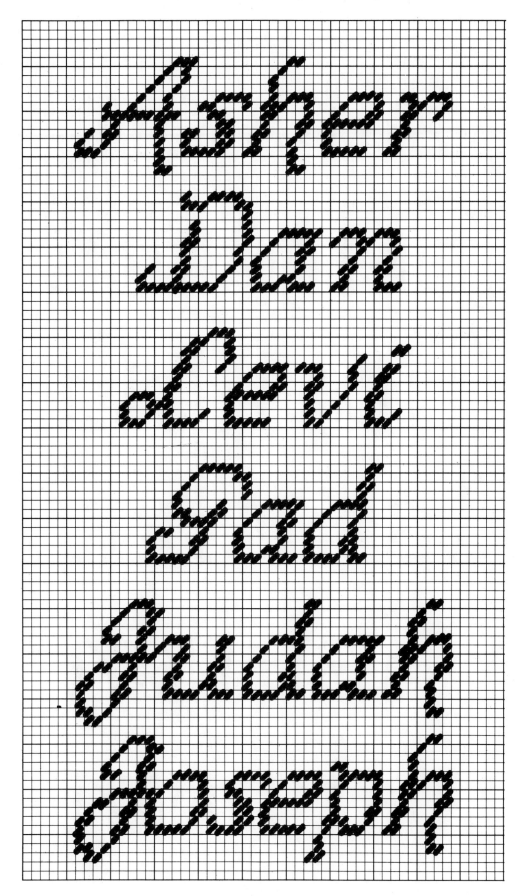

Simeon

Benjamin

Naphtali

Issachar

Reuben

Zebulun

THE FOUR SONS

An "In the Beginning" design opened this section, so it seems proper to conclude it with designs of the four sons who signify the continuity of faith through past centuries and into the future. The story of Passover tells of the four sons— one wise, one wicked, one simple, and one who wits not to ask. What says the Wise Son: "What are the testimonies and laws and behaviors which the Lord, our God, has commanded?" What says the Wicked Son: "Of what use is this service to you?" To you and not to himself. What says the Simple Son: "What is all this about?" But the One Who Wits Not to Ask, it is for thee to open talk with him. "This is an account of what the Lord did for me when I went forth from Egypt."

DATA

#14 canvas

Figures and outline—Mosaic Stitch—2 strands Persian-type Wool

Background—Tent Stitch—2 strands Persian-type Wool

Mat—Double Brick Stitch over 4 and 2 canvas threads—3 strands Persian-type Wool

The figures may also be used for appliqué (fabric or felt) or use them for dolls or hand puppets.

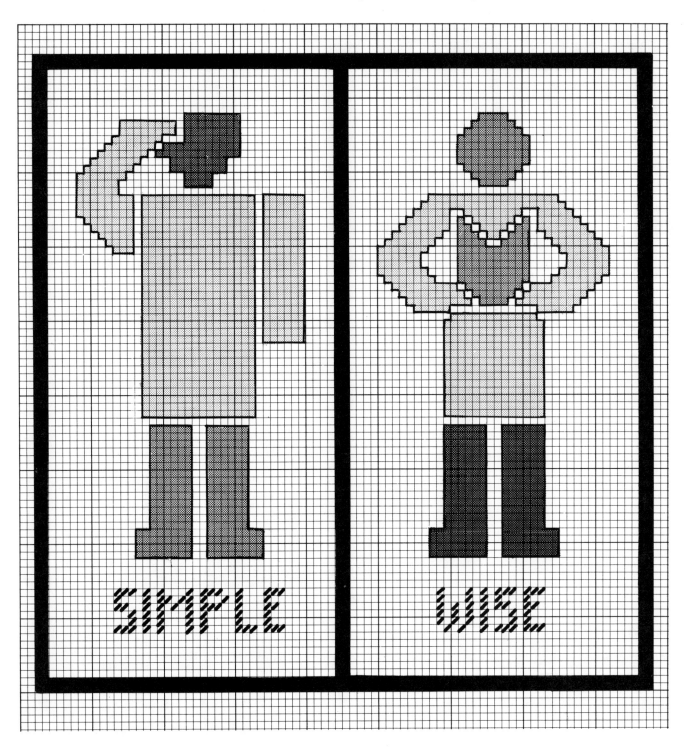

THE FOUR SONS (CONCLUDED)

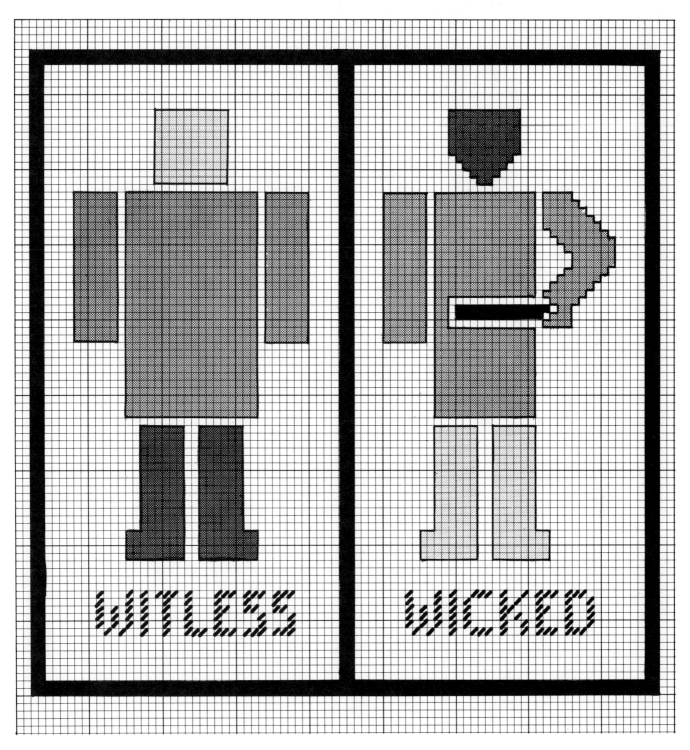

SECTION IV
Antiquity

INTRODUCTION

Because those of the Jewish faith were often described as ''People of the Book,'' their contributions to the world of art were often overlooked. Archaeologists have now found new evidence of their talents as architects and decorators in such places as the synagogues at Dura-Europos, built seventeen hundred years ago, and Bet Alpha, built fourteen hundred years ago. When Moses built his tabernacle his instructions to Bezalel and Oholiab, craftsmen and weavers, were to make it beautiful. Descriptions of the First and Second Temples mention carvings of cherubim, lions, palm trees, flowers, seven-branched candlesticks, ornamented lavers, and other ritualistic objects. Gold and silver vessels were melted down and lost to posterity but mosaic floorings have survived vandalism. Most existing examples were laid down during the Byzantine period, the fifth and sixth centuries C.E.

In those countries that accorded religious freedom during the Middle Ages, Jews worked as artisans, goldsmiths, lacemakers, bookbinders, mapmakers, and calligraphers. Hebrew manuscripts of that period reveal the influences of time and place on Jewish subjects and themes. For example, one can see the differences between German and Spanish styles of illumination.

Styles change, techniques change, but geometrics and formalized representations of trees, flowers, birds, and animals have always been popular for Torah mantle, *paroket* (ark curtain), and *hupah* (wedding canopy), and other ornaments for the synagogue as well as for linens and secular objects for the home.

Women have always practiced the applied arts regardless of time or place. They decorated their own and their family's clothing, their homes, and their table linens with needlework in artistic attempts at self-expression. Usage and time take heavy toll of fabric, so examples of the housewife's talents, designs, and workmanship from the Middle Ages are few, whereas manuscripts—examples of masculine talents—have survived.

Perhaps your own hand-made pieces will be treasured through the years and become the antiques of the future.

MENORAH MIZRAH

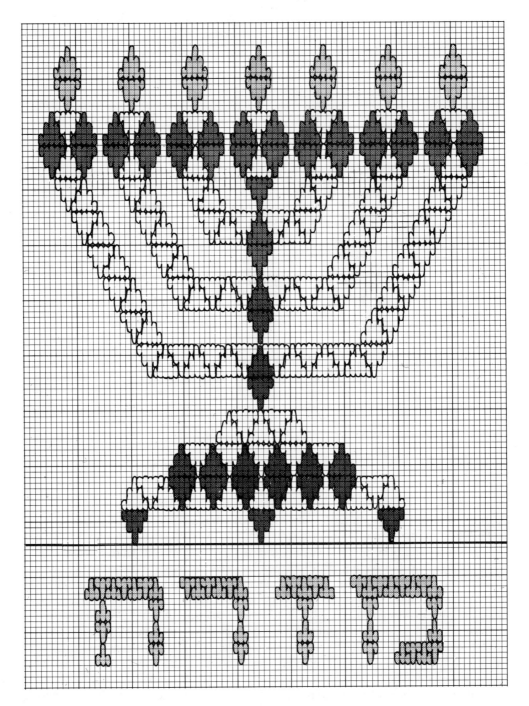

DATA

#10 canvas

Menorah and letters—3 strands
    Persian-type Wool

Background—Brick Stitch over two
    canvas threads

Pedestal—Gobelin Stitch over 2 canvas
    threads—3 strands Persian-type
    Wool

Frame size—8 x 10

This *menorah* design has the same
growth potential as the Grow-Power
Aleph Bet so it is adaptable to any size
project. See the *Chai* Sampler for
methods of enlargement. Here the
menorah uses a 5-stitch unit while the
letters are done in the 3-stitch basic unit
of the Grow-Power *Aleph Bet*.

MENORAH MIZRAH

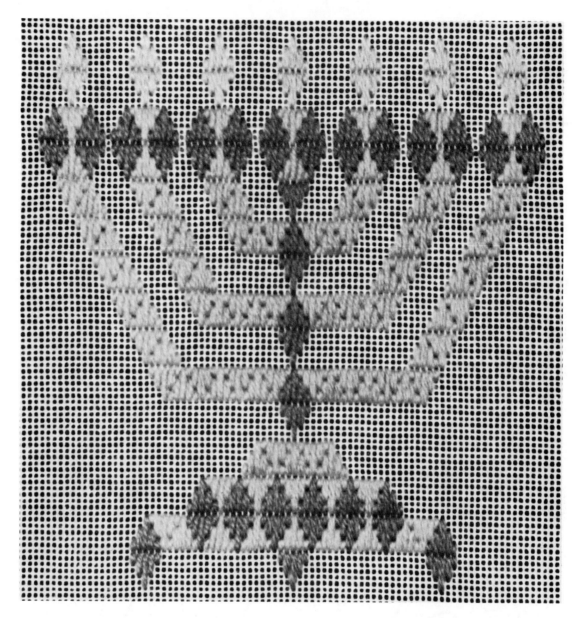

The seven-branched golden candlestick made in accordance with the commandment unto Moses was lit every day until the Temple of Jerusalem was destroyed. It became the symbol of the spiritual values of Judaism. *Mizrah* means "rising of the sun" or "east." When the word is used in a wall hanging or placque, the piece is called a *mizrah* and is hung on the eastern wall of a room to indicate the direction of Jerusalem, the direction faced while praying.

MASSADA MOSAIC PILLOW

This is one quarter of the design. Repeat by turning this portion counterclockwise around the center of the small circle.

MASSADA MOSAIC PILLOW

The Roman legions under Titus sacked Jerusalem in 73 B.C.E. but one small group of rebels held out for three years in the rock fortress of Massada (Masada) near the Dead Sea. They finally killed themselves rather than surrender to the Romans. Their name, Zealots, is now an English word that means "fanatical partisans." The colors used for the pillow approximate those of a mosaic floor in Massada from which the design was adapted.

DATA

#10 canvas—natural color
Stitch—Tent and Mosaic
3 strands Persian-type Wool
Finished size—15 x 15
This is the only example of a painted canvas.
Outlining would have served as well.

MOSAIC PAVEMENT PILLOW

MOSAIC PAVEMENT PILLOW

Geometric designs were in vogue during the fourth century C.E. The mosaic pavement of the Church of Shavei Zion, which was uncovered in the Holy Land in 1955, featured a King Solomon's Knot and a chevron effect within a square which inspired this design. The unfinished piece of needlework shows the Bargello pattern both with and without backstitching done with a single strand of dark grey wool to simulate grouting between tiles. The pattern may be enlarged by doing 4-stitch squares or by increasing the number of chevrons that point to the center.

DATA

#10 canvas
Bargello Stitch over 3 canvas
    threads—3 strands Persian-
    type Wool
Back Stitch—1 strand Persian-
    type Wool
Finished size—10 x 10

COSMETIC CASE AND CREDIT CARD CASE

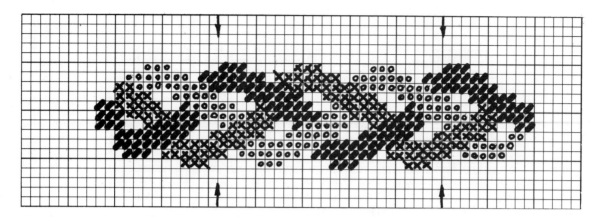

DATA #1

#10 canvas
3 strands Persian-type Wool
Stitch—Tent
Size—1 x 7½

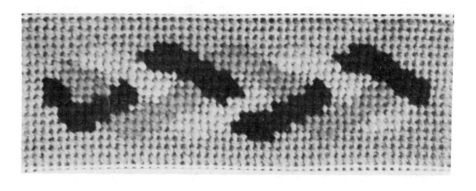

The braid design was used on a credit card case because money means "dough" or "bread." *Hallah* means "dough" and is the name used for the braided bread blessed and served on the Sabbath and Holy Days. Fresh, warm *hallah* is food fit for the gods! A design for a *hallah* cover could incorporate the braid and the blessing in either Hebrew or English, done in Cross Stitch on linen. For a continuous braid repeat the 24-stitch unit between the arrows on the graph.

DATA #2

#12 canvas
3 strands Persian-type Wool
Stitch—Tent
Size—1½ x 5

Rippling wave patterns were favorites with artisans of the second to fourth centuries C.E. Shades of blue on one side of the white crest line and shades of red on the other side were the most popular colors used.

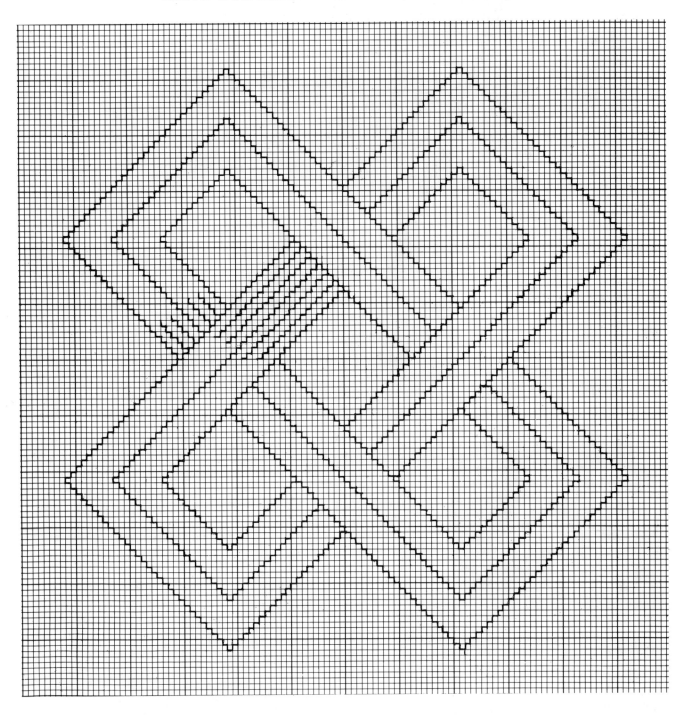

Truth and justice are inseparable as are the links in a motif aptly named King Solomon's Knot. It was often rendered in mosaic chips as in the geometric flooring described on page 93.

KING SOLOMON'S KNOT SHOULDER BAG

DATA

#10 canvas
3 strands Persian-type Wool
Stitch—Bargello over 2 canvas threads, horizontal for
    motif, vertical for background
Finished size—9 x 9

The front of the 11½-square beige velveteen bag
frames a 9-inch-square Bargello piece. One link in the
motif is two shades of beige, the other two shades of rust.
The background is dark grey. The needleworked piece
would also be appropriate on a *tallit* bag for the business-
man or on a book cover or magazine rack in his office or
study.

KING SOLOMON'S KNOT COSMETIC CASE

The Song of Songs
The song of songs, which is Solomon's.
Let him kiss me with the kisses of his mouth
For thy love is better than wine.
Thine ointments have a goodly fragrance;
Behold, thou art fair, my love; behold thou art fair;
Thine eyes are as doves.

KING SOLOMON'S KNOT COSMETIC CASE

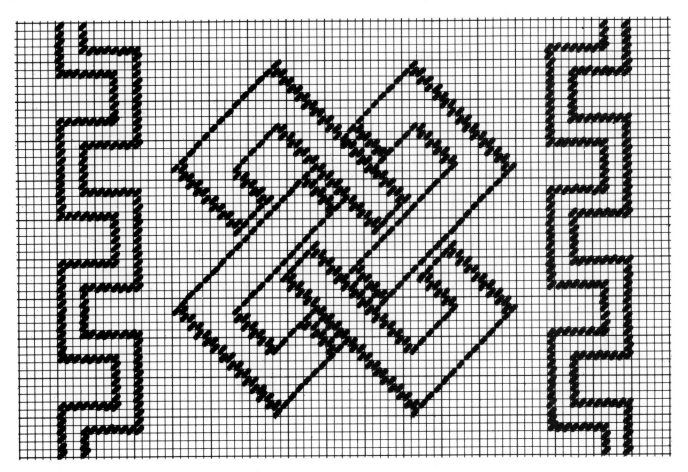

DATA

#12 canvas
3 strands Persian-type Wool
Stitch—Tent
Finished size—4½ x 7

Here King Solomon's Knot is used in a design for a case to hold your lipstick, perfume, and eye makeup. *Behold, thou art fair*. If the knot is done in one color, use at least one row of the ground color to separate the links where they cross to retain the over and under interlacing feature of the motif.

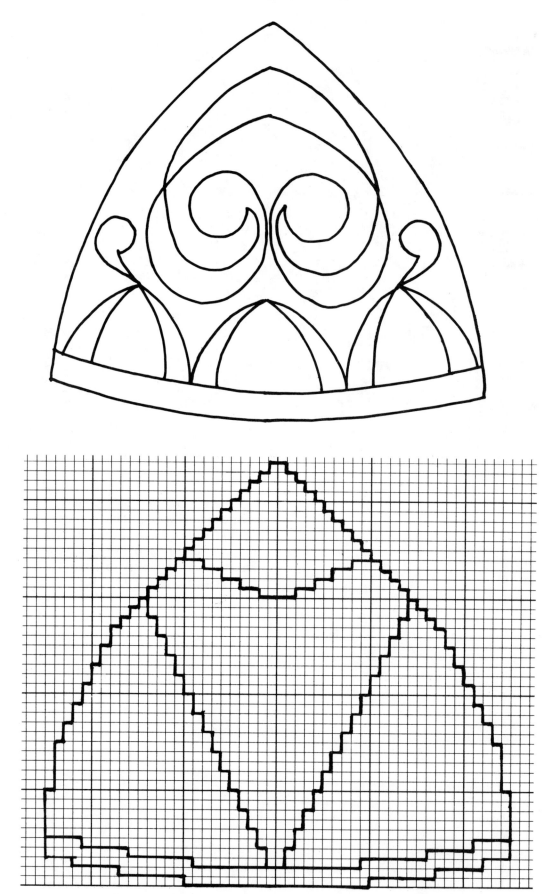

TWO *YARMULKAS*

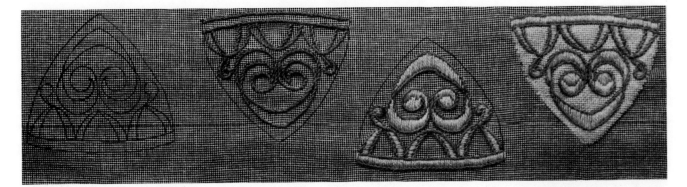

DATA #1

#14 canvas
Outline and Bar-
    gello stitch—3
    strands Persian-
    type Wool
Background—Tent
    Stitch—2
    strands Persian-
    type Wool

DATA #2

#10 canvas
3 strands Persian-
    type Wool

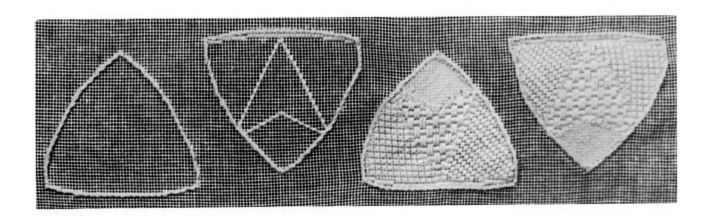

The custom of wearing a headcovering while praying is a matter of social propriety, not religion, but
yarmulkas, skullcaps, or *kippot* (*kippah,* singular; *kip-
piot,* for females) are becoming more popular with
young people and are affectionately called "beanies."
The pink and white one here is for a girl to wear at her
Bat Mitzvah. The design was adapted from a Moroc-
can-Jewish piece of embroidery. The all-white *yar-
mulka* is for a bridegroom. The four areas of each unit
were done in Reverse Basketweave (top), Double Parisian Stitch (middle), and Mosaic Stitch, Straight and
Diagonal. The finished pieces were blocked, cut, hand
sewn together, blocked into a cap shape, and lined.

JACOB'S LADDER BOLSTER PILLOW

Religion was a vital part of the lives of the colonists so it was not strange that the women gave Old Testament names to their patchwork patterns. Some of the more popular designs were called Jacob's Ladder, Joseph's Coat, David and Goliath, Children of Israel, Garden of Eden, King David's Crown, Job's Tears, and Job's Troubles. The first three listed are included here because they are easily adapted to needlepoint canvas. They may be done in Tent Stitch only or worked as stitch samplers like the bolster pillow shown. If sewing is your hobby you may also want to do them in fabrics for items such as *tallit* bags, tote bags, lap robes, pillow tops, vests, skirts, aprons, or wall hangings.

DATA

#10 canvas
3 strands Persian-type Wool
1½"-squares (40)—various stitches
3"-squares of 2 colors (8)—Tent Stitch
Finished size—9 x 18

JACOB'S LADDER (PATTERN)

In a dream Jacob saw angels of God ascending and descending a ladder that reached up to heaven. The "Jacob's Ladder" bolster pillow has a never-ending series of steps that wind 'round and 'round like the stripes on an old-fashioned barber's pole. Three tones of one color are favored for this pattern. Navy blue, medium blue, and white were used for the two 9-inch repeats needed to make the bolster pillow. A different stitch was used in each of the twenty navy and the twenty white squares covering fifteen threads. The medium blue and white squares over thirty canvas threads were done in Tent Stitch. The markings along the edges of the patterns proportion the individual patches and will be helpful when rescaling for sewing or needlepointing.

JACOB'S LADDER (PATTERN)

A second version of the same nine-patch pattern uses only two colors and accentuates the ladder effect. Blue and white is the favorite color combination for this design, perhaps because the "thread of blue" formed by the diagonal is, as described in the Torah, a reminder to follow the commandments of the Lord.

JOSEPH'S COAT (PATTERN)

Jacob gave Joseph a fine coat of many colors which made him the envy of his brothers. Pioneer women used every scrap of usable fabric in a pattern they named Joseph's coat, but in more affluent times the number of different colored patches used was limited to four.

DAVID AND GOLIATH (PATTERN)

Use as few as three colors or as many as you wish in this pattern. Limit stitch choice to one, such as Tent or Bargello, or execute in a variety of stitches.

SECTION V
Contemporary

INTRODUCTION

Throughout the ages women have sought relaxation and self-expression through decorative stitchery, much as you or I would today. This book was specifically intended for those women who want to express themselves and their heritage in needlework.

If at this stage in your needlepoint career you are content to adapt suggested ideas and designs to your own needs in color combinations of your own choice, use the graphs and drawings in this section to exercise and improve your technical skills on that level. The last two offerings, the Knesset *Menorah* and the Seal of Israel, are particularly suited to the limited experience of newer devotees of needlepoint who would like to make reminders of the ties that bind us to the history and spiritual values of the Holy Land.

When the time comes that you feel compelled to put your own creative ideas into execution, you will enter new, exciting, stimulating territories. You will look at designs in a different way, seeing not only with your eyes but with your imagination too, both assessing and relating on a more personal level. The design in front of you may gain a different aura, or it may assume an entirely different shape in your mind's eye, or it may be that catalyst that brings a dormant, nebulous idea into full bloom. Capture and nurture that creative line of thought—the chess board suggested by the *Shalom* pillow, the New Year's card with a photograph of your Knesset Menorah piece—to find self-expression in your needlework.

SHALOM PLACQUE

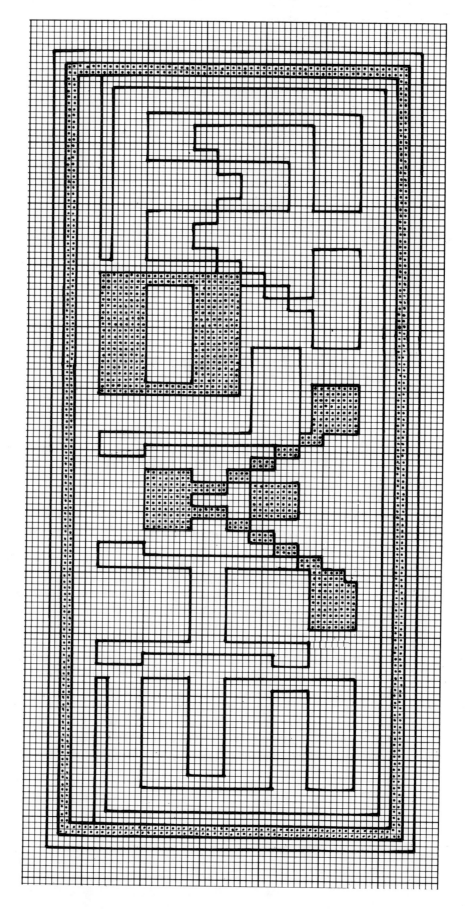

SHALOM PLACQUE

DATA

#12 canvas

Letters and borders—Mosaic Stitch—3 strands
Persian-type Wool

Background—Tent Stitch—2 strands Persian-type
Wool

Finished size—5 x 11

Here is an easy-to-count project for your leisure time. When finished and hanging in your front hall it will say "Welcome" to your guests. The letter shapes feature the strong horizontal bars and thin vertical lines that distinguish ancient Hebrew script from Roman lettering. Different colored letters bring interest and legibility to the message.

GOURMET OR *KOSHER* KITCHEN

When you have done needlepoint for every other room in your house, you may want an example of your expertise for your *kosher* kitchen or for a Gentile friend. The letter "U" in a circle is the symbol for "in accordance with Jewish dietary laws."

DATA

#10 canvas
3 strands Persian-type Wool
Stitch—Tent
Finished size—7½ x 18

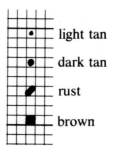

light tan
dark tan
rust
brown

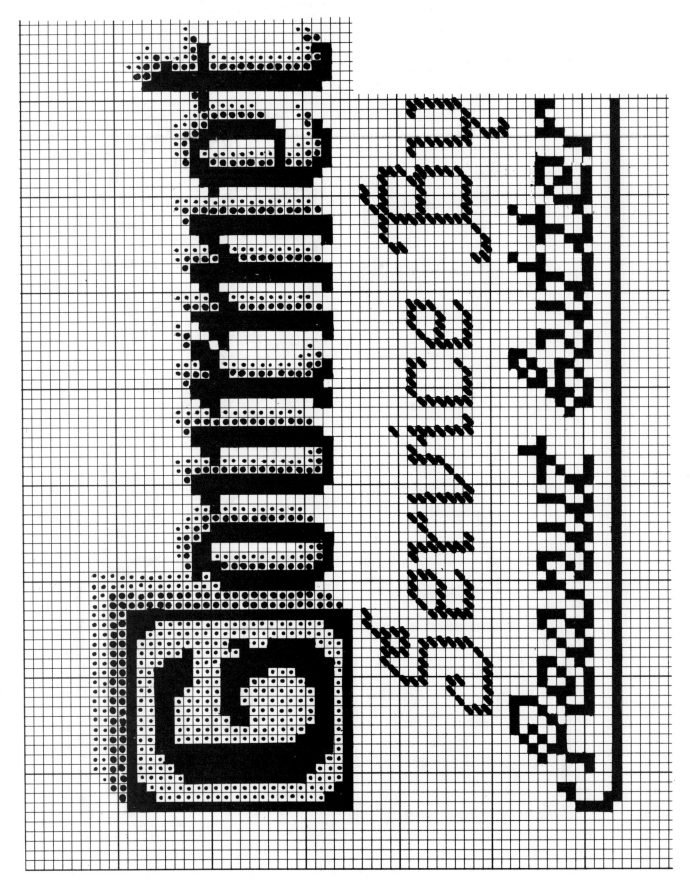

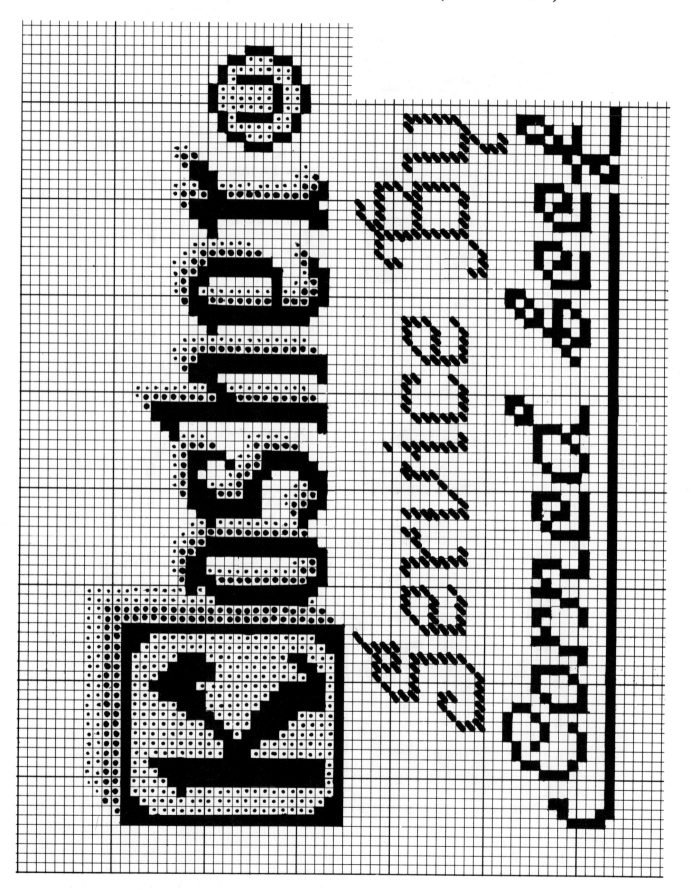

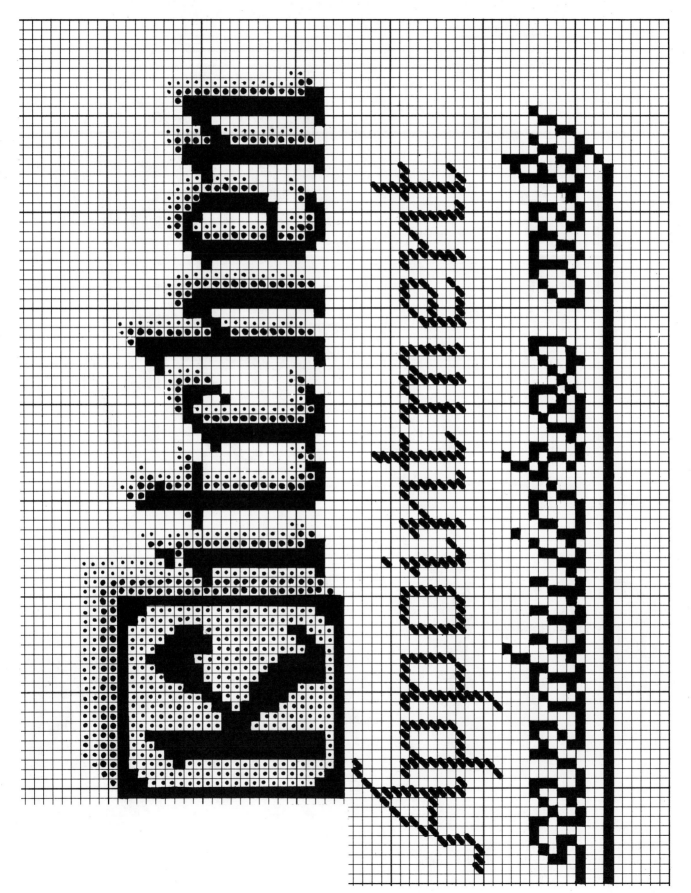

STARS-IN-YOUR-EYES SPECTACLE CASE

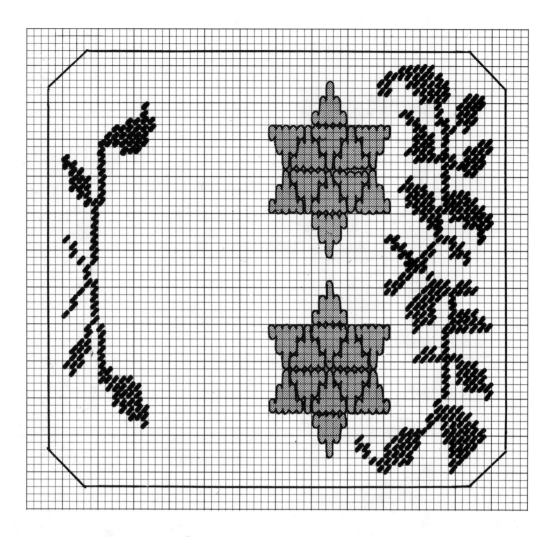

The Star of David is used in a variety of ways on a variety of gift items because it is the most popular identifying motif in contemporary Jewish applied arts. Here two stars are all-seeing eyes under laurel leaf eyebrows and above a smiling mouth.

DATA

#10 canvas
3 strands Persian-type Wool
Stitch—Tent with Bargello for the stars only
Finished size—5½ x 6½

SHALOM PILLOW

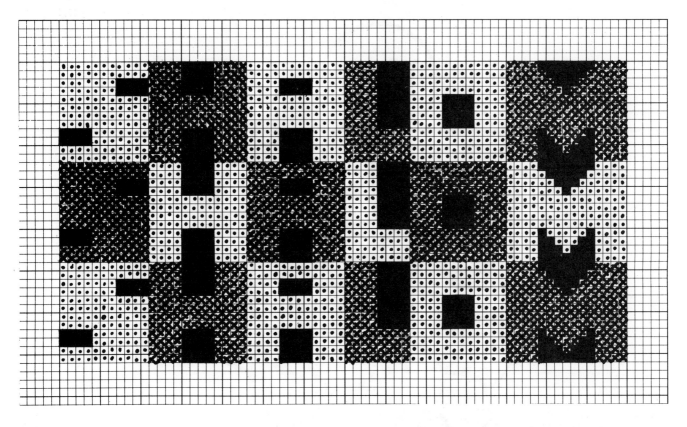

DATA

#5 Penelope canvas
Letters—5 stitches to the inch—Tent Stitch—Acrylic rug
  yarn
Background—10 stitches to the inch—Tent Stitch—
  Arcylic sport yarn
Finished size—14 x 14

Repetition of a letter or letters is a simple, effective way to create an endless number of space and color patterns. Use block letters (English as shown or Hebrew such as size 15 *Aleph Bet*) to experiment in this fascinating type of geometric designing.

PEACE—nothing is perfect. The error in the needlework was discovered and corrected when the background was being done.

GRAPE TRAY

GRAPE TRAY

Two of the spies sent by Moses to reconnoiter the promised land returned with gigantic clusters of grapes carried on a stave between them.

The Jewish calender year 5738 ended in 1978. A difference of 3760 and a repetition of the final numeral should be maintained if the dates are changed.

DATA

#12 canvas

Grapes—outlined in Tent Stitch, filled in with a selection of pattern stitches—2 or 3 strands Persian-type Wool to suit conditions

Leaves, numerals, and background—Tent Stitch—2 strands Persian-type Wool

Finished size—5 x 12

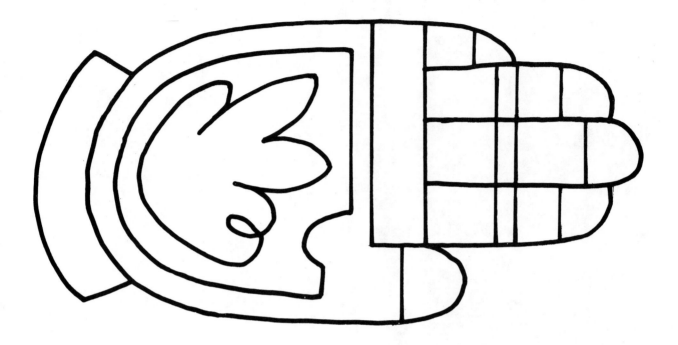

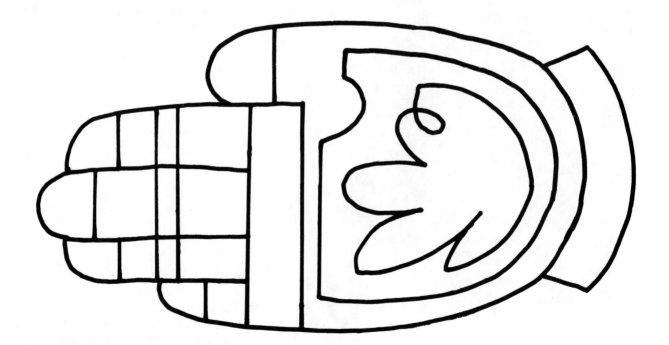

HAMSA PILLOW

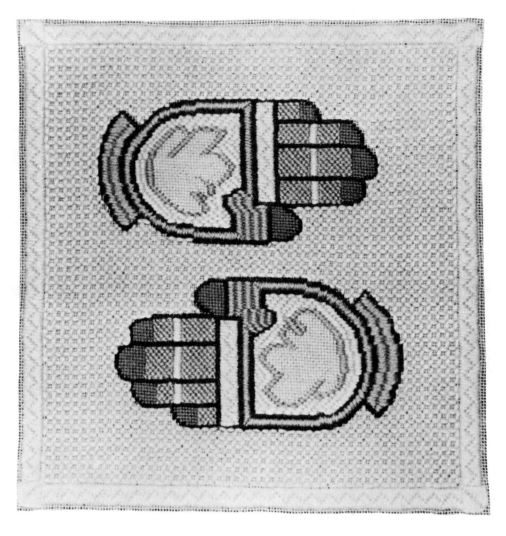

A *hamsa* is an amulet shaped like a hand. For centuries it has been a popular Middle Eastern charm to ward off evil and now, made up in silver filagree, it is a favorite Israeli souvenir item.

DATA

#14 canvas—natural color
2 strands Persian-type Wool
Stitches—Tent, Brick, and Bargello
Background—Punch stitch over 3 canvas threads

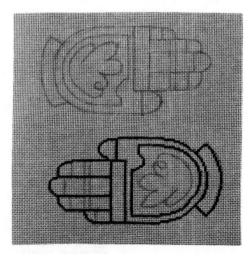

The outlines were traced on canvas and worked in Tent Stitch. Red was used for the finger nails. Bargello and Brick Stitches fill in the motif to capture the look of filagree. Fast-working Punch Stitch covers the background for a delicate-appearing but sturdy fabric, the back being covered by Cross Stitches.

KNESSET MENORAH

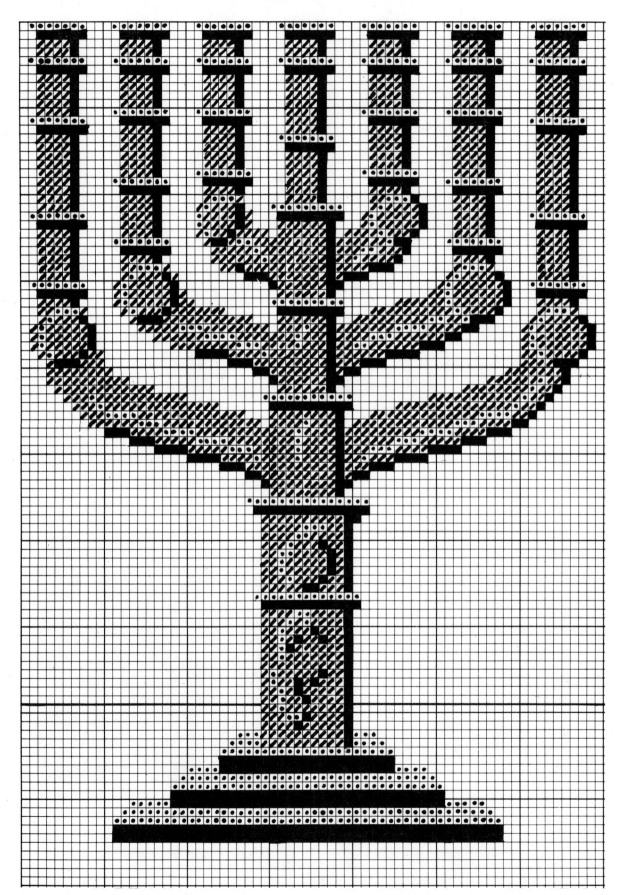

KNESSET MENORAH

DATA

#12 canvas
2 strands Persian-type Wool
Stitch—Tent Stitch for design and background—Long-armed Cross Stitch for
foreground
Frame—8 x 10

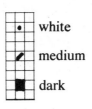

- white
- medium
- dark

The big bronze *menorah* that stands outside
Israel's Knesset (House of Representatives) is
the work of Benno Elkan and the gift of the
British Parliament. It is decorated with scenes
from biblical history and is an impressive symbol of Judaic culture.

SEAL OF ISRAEL

DATA

#14 canvas
2 strands Persian-type Wool
Emblem—Tent Stitch
Title—Cross Stitch
Mat—Diagonal Scotch Stitch
Frame—8 x 10

The final design offering is a simplified version of the seal of Israel above the date of its creation as a Jewish State.

STITCH IDENTIFICATION

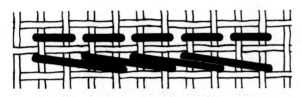

Back Stitch
Outline Stitch

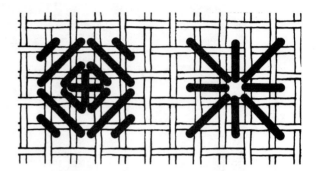

Mosaic Blocks with Upright Cross
Star Stitch

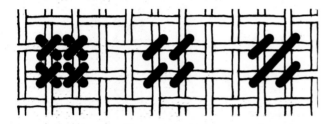

Cross Stitch
Tent, Half Cross, Continental or Basketweave
Mosaic Stitch

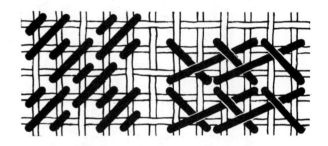

Diagonal Mosaic
Plait or Long Armed Cross Stitch

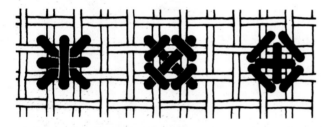

Double Cross or Smyrna Stitch
Rice Stitch
Upright Cross with Diagonals

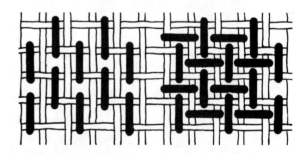

Brick Stitch
Reverse Basketweave Stitch

Scotch Stitch
Cubed Cross, Double Leviathan or Rhodes Stitch

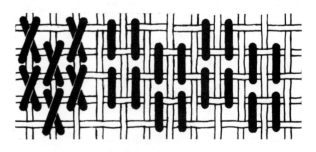

Long Cross Stitch
Double Brick Stitch

STITCH IDENTIFICATION

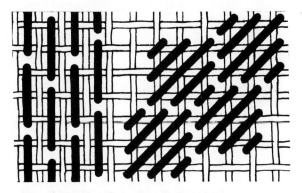

Bargello or Florentine Stitch
Diagonal Scotch Stitch

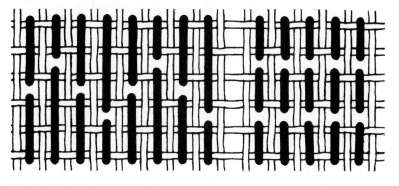

Bargello Border Stitch
Gobelin Stitch

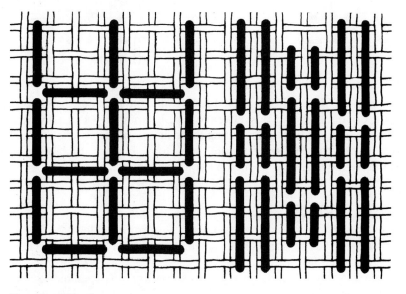

Punch Stitch
Double Parisian Stitch

Instructions and Useful Hints

CONCERNING GRAPHS

Each square of a graph represents the intersection of a horizontal and a vertical thread of a canvas.
COUNT SPACES OF A GRAPH - COUNT THREADS OF A CANVAS

In this book the name "Tent Stitch" is used generically and includes the look-alike stitches known as Tent, Half Cross, Continental, and Basketweave. The last named was used wherever possible in the needlework shown. If you need help in executing these or any of the stitches named and illustrated on pages 124 and 125 or want to increase your stitch repertoire, borrow stitch manuals from your public library before you make a decision as to the one you want to own and use.

CONCERNING CANVAS

Allow generous borders of canvas when you plan your project, at least 2 to 2½ inches on each side. You will never be sorry for having done so but you may regret not being able to recenter your motif or add a border to your original layout.

To determine the size of a design shown on 10-to-an-inch graph paper and executed on

        #10 canvas - multiply by 1
        #12 canvas - multiply by 5/6
        #14 canvas - multiply by 5/7
        #16 canvas - multiply by 5/8
        #18 canvas - multiply by 5/9
        # 5 canvas - multiply by 2
        # 4 canvas - multiply by 2½.

To determine the selvedge edge of a piece of Mono canvas without selvedge edge, pull a thread off any edge. If it is wavy, it is a warp (parallel to selvedge) thread. If it is straight, it is a weft thread that extended from selvedge to selvedge.

Do not do Half Cross Stitch on Mono canvas because it will not hold this stitch in place. If you plan to use Half Cross Stitch, as was done on the Block *Aleph Bet* Pillow, use Interlocking or Penelope canvas.

CONCERNING YARN

Always select or match colors in daylight. If this is impossible in the shop you patronize, reassess your choice in daylight before you start your project.

Never use ripped-out yarn.

If you have trouble threading your needle, try this method: cut a strip of paper narrower than the eye of the needle and about 1 inch long. Fold to ½ inch long, place the yarn inside the fold, push the two ends of the paper through the needle's eye and then pull the yarn through.

After threading your needle, run your thumb and forefinger along each end of the yarn from the needle out toward the end. You will feel that one is smoother, less scratchy than the other. The end that is smoother to the touch should be the longer and worked into the canvas.

Straight stitches such as Brick, Bargello, Florentine, and Gobelin require thicker yarn or more strands of Persian-type wool to cover the threads of a canvas than do slanted stitches.

Strands of yarn kept flat and parallel will cover canvas better and give a more beautiful texture than when allowed to twist. Untwist your yarn by allowing your threaded needle to dangle below your work once in a while.

Keep some strands of each of the colors used in your project and tag them with color number or description of piece for which it was used. The color of yarn in strands and of yarn in stitches will seem different and make matching colors more difficult.

CONCERNING EXECUTION

The use of a frame will minimize canvas distortion.

When executing an intricate pattern from a graph, it may be easier to outline large areas first and fill them in later.

When filling in an area, try to follow a procedure that allows you to draw your yarn *down* through an occupied hole and *up* through an empty hole of the canvas.

But when both dark and light colors are to share holes in a canvas, put in the lighter color first, if possible. Then, through a shared hole, pull the dark yarn up from the back of the canvas, taking care to avoid splitting the light-colored yarn already in the hole. Draw the dark yarn down through an empty hole. This sequence will carry dark fuzz or lint to the back of the canvas, away from the light-colored yarn on the top surface and thus help ensure a sharp, clear line between colors.

When doing Cross Stitch, always cross in the same direction.

When Bargello and Tent Stitches are next to each other, Tent Stitches should share holes used by the Bargello Stitch and also occupy the holes under the long straight stitch so that canvas threads will will not remain exposed where the two types of stitches meet.

When planning the spacing of Hebrew letters, follow the same rules used for English letters: keep round letters close together and allow more space between vertical strokes. Try to maintain equal negative areas (background space) between and around letters.

Follow manufacturer's instructions when using marking pens and canvas paints. The important thing is that they be waterproof. Test them before you do your needlework.

FINAL ITEM

Initial or sign and date your piece. In years to come you will be glad you did.

Bibliography

Ausubel, Nathan. *Pictorial History of the Jewish People.* New York: Crown Publishers, 1975.

Borssuck, B. *97 Needlepoint Alphabets.* New York: Arco Publishing, Inc., 1975.

Davidovitch, David. *The Ketuba, Jewish Marriage Contracts Through the Ages.* Tel-Aviv: E. Lewin-Epstein Ltd., Publishers, 1968.

Dayan, Ruth with Feinberg, Wilburt. *Crafts of Israel.* New York: MacMillan Publishing Co., Inc., 1974.

Hall, Carrie A. and Kretsinger, Rose G. *The Romance of the Patchwork Quilt in America.* New York: Crown Publishers, 1935.

Israeli Mosaics of the Byzantine Period. New York: New American Library of World Literature, Inc.

Kushner, Lawrence. *The Book of Letters.* New York: Harper and Row, Publishers, 1975.

The Jewish Catalog. Philadelphia: The Jewish Publication Society of America, 1973.

The Junior Jewish Encyclopedia. New York: Shengold Publishers, Inc., 1957.

Lantz, Sherlee. *Trianglepoint* New York: The Viking Press, 1976.

Lantz, Sherlee and Lane, Maggie A. *A Pageant of Pattern for Needlepoint Canvas.* New York: Grosset and Dunlap, Inc., 1975.

Narkiss, Bezalel. *Hebrew Illuminated Manuscripts.* Jerusalem: Encyclopaedia Judaica, 1969.

Rockland, Mae Shafter. *The Work of Our Hands.* New York: Schocken Books, 1973.

Toby, L.F. *The Art of Hebrew Lettering.* Tel Aviv: Cosmopolite Ltd., 1976.